EVERYDAY FAMILY RECIPES FOR YOUR COMBINATION MICROWAVE

Carolyn Humphries

A How To Book

ROBINSON

ROBINSON

First published in Great Britain in 2015 by Robinson

Copyright © Carolyn Humphries, 2015

The moral right of the author has been asserted.

A CIP catalogue record for this book
is available from the British Library.

ISBN: 978-1-47213-560-5 (paperback)
ISBN: 978-1-47213-561-2 (ebook)

Typeset by Basement Press, Glaisdale
Printed and bound in Great Britain by CPI Group (UK) Ltd,
Croydon CR0 4YY

Papers used by Robinson are from well-managed forests
and other sustainable sources

MIX
Paper from
responsible sources
FSC® C104740

Robinson
is an imprint of
Little, Brown Book Group
Carmelite House
50 Victoria Embankment
London EC4Y 0DZ

An Hachette UK Company
www.hachette.co.uk

www.littlebrown.co.uk

How To Books are published by Robinson, an imprint of Little, Brown Book
Group. We welcome proposals from authors who have first-hand experience of
their subjects. Please set out the aims of your book, its target market and its
suggested contents in an email to Nikki.Read@howtobooks.co.uk

CONTENTS

INTRODUCTION

A combination cooker is a microwave, convection oven and grill in one. Each can be used separately or the speed of the microwave combined with either of the other two forms of cooking. It can become your best friend in the kitchen, cooking delicious and nutritious meals quickly and efficiently without you having to slave over a hot stove for hours. So ditch the ready meals, have takeaways as a special treat only and say hello to a healthier, tastier lifestyle for all the family.

The microwave has been a great accessory in the kitchen for many years – making it easy to prepare many foods more quickly than in a conventional cooker. However, it doesn't brown food (unless it contains lots of fat or sugar, which caramelise naturally as it cooks). While this is perfect for some foods, such as soups, risottos, steamed or stewed dishes, it's not ideal for anything which requires a nice brown finish. It will not tenderise food either, as with roasts or slow-cooked casseroles, and is no good for any baking, such as gratins, breads, pies and scones.

A combination cooker can change all that. You have the microwaves to speed up the cooking process, but you can combine these, when appropriate, with the convection oven or grill to give dishes the appetising crisp and brown appearance finish we all love; in some cases, you can use it to tenderise the food too.

All the great-tasting recipes in this book are simple to prepare and very easy to cook. Some dishes simply require microwaving alone and others need only the convection oven, but many require the combination of microwave and convection or microwave and grill.

Now you may think that if a recipe only requires convection cooking, you might as well use your conventional oven. However, if you are making only one dish, the compact-sized oven in your combination cooker will use far less fuel and is therefore more cost-efficient. You may also believe it to be a bit of a bother to juggle dishes – cooking different elements of your meal one after the other – as is required for a few of the recipes. I thought that, too. But in reality it's not that different from juggling pots and pans on the hob, or moving things in and out of your conventional oven because they cook at different times. Also, if you use a microwave, the food needs to stand anyway – covered with foil or a lid – to allow the heat to distribute evenly throughout (*see* standing time, page 9) – so it will remain hot while the second part of the meal cooks.

Nevertheless, it would be daft to be a slave to the combination cooker and not use it in conjunction with your hob when it's more practical to do so. For instance, when I'm roasting a chicken and then potatoes in my combination oven, I put a green vegetable to cook on the hob when the potatoes are nearly ready rather than waiting for them to be ready and the microwave to be free to cook the greens. The more you use your combination cooker, the more you'll get used to it and work out how best to utilise it to suit your needs.

Another big plus is that cooking rapidly as in a microwave or combination cooker preserves nutrients, making it a healthier way to cook. Here you'll find easy-to-make, mouthwatering recipes for everything from breakfasts to main meals, snacks and side dishes to desserts, sauces, breads, cakes and preserves. You can cook with confidence, happy in the knowledge you are creating healthy meals for your family while also using less fuel – which in turn helps our planet as well as your bank balance!

USING YOUR COMBINATION MICROWAVE

My combination cooker has a powerful 1000-watt microwave. Yours may have a slightly lower wattage, so always check your manufacturer's instruction manual as cooking times may need to be extended slightly. As with other methods, cooking in this way is not an exact science because different brands of oven vary slightly – always keep an eye on and check your food before the end of cooking. You can always add a little more time but you can't rectify an overcooked dish!

My oven has a metal tray to use when grilling, convection or combination cooking, to heat the food from underneath as the heating element (the grill) is at the top of the oven. Some other machines have an element top and bottom, and so provide a low rack to put food on to avoid placing it directly on the element. In the recipes here, I have therefore instructed to place your dish on the metal tray or low rack on the turntable. However, some models don't have a turntable at all. These are particularly good for convection-only cooking, as there is a larger surface area on which to place a dish (it goes directly on the base of the oven and doesn't need to have room to turn). You can therefore use bigger dishes. But, if microwaving, you may need to turn food manually for even results. Always check your own manufacturer's instructions and follow them if they differ from mine.

MICROWAVING

OVEN TEMPERATURES

Combination microwaves, annoyingly, don't all use the same terminology for microwave oven power, so I have tried to standardise and give you the percentage power as well. My oven, for instance, has LOW as 440 watts, which is about 45 per cent power, and has WARM as 10 per cent, but most have LOW as 10 per cent. So, please go by the percentage power and do double-check the terminology for your own cooker.

For reference, throughout this book I have listed oven temperatures as follows:

HIGH: 100 per cent power
MEDIUM-HIGH: 70 per cent power
MEDIUM: 50–60 per cent power
MEDIUM-LOW/SIMMER: 25–30 per cent power
LOW/WARM: 10 per cent power

HOW MICROWAVES WORK

In a conventional cooker, the heat is radiated round the food cooking it from the outside inwards. This gives the brown cooked appearance we are all familiar with. Microwaves, however, agitate water molecules in the food and this friction produces heat and cooks the food.

It is important to use the right containers when cooking in a microwave. Utensils containing metal reflect the microwaves, which bounce off the surface and cause 'arcing' – sparks to fly. Apart from causing damage to your cooker, this would prevent the microwaves penetrating the food and cooking it. Porous dishes, such as unglazed earthenware, will absorb moisture from the food. This moisture attracts some of the microwaves, making the dish hot, instead of all the microwaves concentrating on cooking the food and the cooking will take much longer (*see* suitable containers, page 19).

Because there is no external heat source, food in a microwave does not brown in the conventional way. The exceptions are foods high in sugar or fat, which naturally caramelise if they are cooked long enough. That's why you have to keep an eye on some foods, such as sugary cakes, biscuits and fatty bacon, as they can still burn even without the external heat. Some foods don't react well to microwaving (*see* page 16). These are best cooked by convection only.

BROWNING AGENTS

You can 'cheat' when microwave cooking to give a brown appearance to food, for example by brushing with soy or barbecue sauce, sprinkling with paprika or using brown sugar instead of white in cakes. Or by adding a brown crust, such as toasted breadcrumbs or chopped toasted nuts. But with a combination cooker there's no need to add these, unless for flavour or texture, as you have the advantage of being able to use a grill or convection heat to brown the outside while the inside cooks quicker than in a conventional oven.

ARRANGING FOOD ON THE TURNTABLE

How you arrange food in the microwave is important. If cooking unevenly shaped foods, such as broccoli or chicken legs, arrange around the outside of a dish with the densest parts facing outwards. Individual items, such as jacket potatoes or cupcakes, should also be placed in a circle round the edge of the turntable. Even-sized pieces, such as sliced carrots, should be spread out in an even layer in the dish so they all get blasted with the same amount of microwaves. Although the turntable helps, you will need to stir or rearrange food where possible during cooking to make sure it receives an even distribution of microwaves (obviously this doesn't apply to baked dishes that need to cook in one piece).

QUANTITIES

The most important thing to remember is: the more food in the microwave, the longer it takes to cook. So, for instance, if you want to microwave one jacket potato, it will take 4–5 minutes (depending on size), two will take 7–8 minutes and four about 13 minutes. However, if you just want to melt a small amount of chocolate or, say, heat enough frozen peas for one portion, it's best to put a cup of water in the microwave alongside the food. This absorbs some of the microwaves which would otherwise bounce around, unable to target such a small quantity of food.

WHEN COOKING FOR ONE ON MICROWAVE ONLY

Quarter all the ingredients, use a smaller dish and cook for a quarter of the time. You will probably need to cook a little longer. It's likely to take a third of the time rather than a quarter, but it's better to check then cook a little more rather than ruin the dish by overcooking.

STANDING TIME

Whenever you cook using microwaves, the food requires standing time to complete the cooking process. The vibrating water molecules don't simply stop when the microwave switches off: they continue to vibrate causing heat and so cooking the food until they gradually slow down and stop. Therefore foods that can easily overcook, such as scrambled eggs or cakes, need to still be slightly moist when they're taken out. They will finish cooking during the standing time. The time necessary is stated in each recipe (though it won't matter if you leave it a little longer). Always cover the food either with foil or leave it covered with its lid if in a casserole or similar dish. I tend to put a tea towel or pair of oven gloves over the lid too, for extra insulation. This standing time allows you to keep the food hot while cooking an accompaniment, such as rice, potatoes or a green vegetable, or to warm bread to serve with the dish.

CONVECTION COOKING

You can use your cooker as a normal little fan oven. It incorporates the heating element (or elements if your oven has one top and bottom) and a fan to circulate the heat around the food. Always ensure you use the metal tray, or the low rack if your oven has one. For best results when using convection only, always preheat the oven, following your manufacturer's instructions.

If you need to open the door during cooking, press the open/release pad and not the stop/start one or the programme will be cancelled, and if you press start again without reprogramming, it will revert to microwave cooking.

As long as you don't intend to use any microwave energy at all, you can use the same cookware you would use in a conventional oven, but don't forget to use oven gloves because the dishes as well as the food and surrounding areas will become as hot, as they would in your in your conventional oven.

GRILLING

You can use your oven as a compact grill for cooking sausages, bacon, chops, toast or anything you would cook under your conventional grill. Always follow your manufacturer's instructions but, in general, if your oven has them, always have the metal tray on the turntable with the high rack in place. Food can be placed directly on the rack, or on the metal tray on top of the rack, in the same way you would use your conventional grill pan. If your oven does not provide a metal tray, you can use a baking sheet or tray that will fit on the rack on the turntable as long as it doesn't touch the sides of the oven as the turntable revolves. Obviously, if your oven does not have a turntable, then you have the whole space in the oven but, again, any container should not touch the sides.

Do not cover food when grilling and always use oven gloves to remove it. There is no need to preheat the grill before use. When grilling alone without microwaving, you can use the same cookware as you would under your normal grill.

Most ovens have three grill settings:

- HIGH (1): The hottest setting, for bacon, chops, sausages, rare or medium-rare steaks, and for toasting bread, crumpets etc.
- MEDIUM (2): For foods that are more delicate or require longer cooking, such as chicken portions, well-done steaks and fish.
- LOW (3): Manufacturers say this can be used like MEDIUM (2) for delicate and longer grilling but, to be honest, I have never used this setting!

COMBINATION COOKING

There are two combinations: convection plus microwave or grill plus microwave. You can also set them manually. So, for instance, if you cook a dish on microwave only on the turntable, you can then put in the metal tray, if necessary, and the high rack if the dish will fit on it, and finish off a dish under the grill to brown. The more you use the cooker, the more adept you will become at using it to suit your cooking. The most important thing is not to try and cook tiny amounts by this method – 200g is the minimum.

CONVECTION PLUS MICROWAVE

This method gives you the best of both worlds: a conventional crisp brown outside along with the speedy cooking of microwaving. Use for casseroles; meat joints, chops and steaks; whole birds and portions; jacket potatoes; baked dishes, such as lasagne; pies, pastries and some cakes.

- You can use any microwave-safe, ovenproof dishes in combination cooking, and also metal bakeware (*see* suitable containers, page 19) providing they are smooth with no seams.
- There is no need to preheat the oven when cooking on combination unless you are cooking pastry.
- Food should be placed on the metal tray or the low rack on the turntable; always use oven gloves to remove after cooking.
- Don't overcrowd food on the metal tray or when using a baking sheet on the rack. If cooking a lot of small cakes, for

instance, it's better to cook in two batches, though you can stop the programme (using the door release pad, not stop/start) and rearrange them so that those browning more slowly are swapped with those that are cooking faster, then press stop/start to continue the programme.

FOODS UNSUITABLE FOR THE CONVECTION PLUS
MICROWAVE TREATMENT
- Thin biscuits (those cooked in a slab, such as shortbread, are fine)
- Meringues or other foods containing whisked egg whites
- Rich fruit cakes
- Yorkshire puddings

CONVERTING RECIPES

In my experience, when converting your own recipes to combination cooking, you need to think as you would when using only microwave power. If a food would spoil when blasted with a lot of microwaves, it will on combination too, so go for a small percentage of microwave power with the convection at a similar temperature to conventional cooking. The cooking time will still be considerably reduced, so check frequently. It will be a case of trial and error, but the easiest way is to find a similar recipe in this book and apply the same principles.

I have found that foods with a high sugar or fat content brown incredibly quickly even at lower temperatures, so you need to watch out for over-browning. If absolutely necessary, lay a smooth sheet of foil over the food towards the end of cooking to prevent this, but you must makes sure that the foil does not touch the sides of the oven at all. Should any arcing (sparks flashing) occur when doing this, remove the foil immediately.

GRILL PLUS MICROWAVE

This is suitable for foods that would normally be grilled, or for reheating small savoury items, such a sausage rolls. It is not necessary to preheat the grill and the food should always be left uncovered. The grill does not remain red throughout cooking; it will glow on and off.

Place food either directly on the high rack, set on the metal tray if your oven has one, on the turntable, or it can be placed on the metal tray or a baking sheet, then set on the rack on the turntable (depending on the food, as you would with normal grilling). Use only cookware suitable for grilling; never use any form of plastic even if microwave-safe (*see* suitable containers, page 19).

As for combination cooking, if food needs turning or rearranging, always open the door using the door-release pad not stop/start. When you close the door, press start and the timing will continue as before.

SUITABLE CONTAINERS FOR MICROWAVING OR COMBINATION COOKING

As I said before, not all containers and cooking wraps are suitable for use when microwaving (but if using the grill or convection oven only, treat it as a conventional cooker).

THE MICROWAVE DISH TEST
If you are unsure whether a dish is suitable for use when microwaving, stand a cup of water alongside the dish on the turntable and MICROWAVE on HIGH for 1 minute. If the water is getting hot but the dish feels cool, it is safe. If the dish is heating up it is absorbing the microwaves, so is not suitable.

OVEN GLASS
Pyrex and similar glass ovenproof dishes, jugs and plates are ideal when using your cooker on microwave, convection or combination. DO NOT USE FOR GRILLING UNLESS FLAMEPROOF. Do not use any fine glass dishes or they may crack.

POTTERY, EARTHENWARE, STONEWARE
If glazed, these are suitable for all cooking in your combination cooker. However, avoid using unglazed dishes when microwaving as they will absorb moisture, which will in turn absorb microwaves, meaning the food will take much longer to cook.

CERAMIC AND CHINA
Providing they are marked as heat-resistant, these can be used. Avoid any with a metal trim when microwaving as they may

cause arcing (sparks) which might damage the magnetron in the microwave. Only use flameproof dishes under the grill. Fine bone china can be used for heating very briefly (such as reheating a cuppa) but do not use for longer cooking periods.

SILICONE BAKEWARE

This is ideal for use in your combination cooker for microwaving and convection cooking. These containers are particularly useful as they are non-stick, so food can simply be popped out after cooking.

WOOD AND BASKETS

Use soaked wooden skewers not metal ones for kebabs in your combination cooker. Soak them for at least an hour in cold water to prevent burning. Wooden bowls and baskets can be used to reheat bread etc. in the microwave, but do not use for cooking in any mode.

FOIL AND METAL CONTAINERS

Use for grilling, convection and some combination cooking only. DO NOT USE WHEN MICROWAVING ONLY OR THEY MAY DAMAGE YOUR COOKER. If using metal baking tins when combination cooking, they must be smooth with no seams: enamel-coated roasting tins are fine and solid cakes tins too. DO NOT USE loose-bottomed or spring-form tins as they have ridges and seams that may cause arcing in the microwave.

ALUMINIUM FOIL

Don't wrap food in foil when microwaving. Tiny strips of smooth foil may be used to shield tips of bones or thin ends of fish when defrosting or microwave cooking to prevent them overcooking or burning. However, make sure the foil does not touch the sides or top of the cooker or it may cause arcing and damage the oven. You can, of course, use it when convection cooking only, and smooth foil can be used to cover food that is over-browning when combination cooking, but make sure the foil does not touch the sides of the oven.

CLING FILM

Microwave-safe cling film can be used to cover a dish when microwaving. Make sure that it is pierced in several places or rolled back slightly at one edge to allow steam to escape, when cooking or reheating. HOWEVER, the food should not come into direct contact with the film. DO NOT USE FOR ANY OTHER MODE OF COOKING.

ROASTER BAGS

These can be used when microwaving meat joints or a whole chicken to help them brown during cooking. Put the meat on a microwave rack or upturned plate in the bag so the juices collect away from the meat. DO NOT USE METAL TIES, only plastic ones.

BASIC FOOD HYGIENE

A cook that's aware of hygiene will help keep the family healthy, so please bear in mind the following when preparing food:

- Always wash your hands before you start.
- Always wash and dry fresh produce before use.
- Don't lick your fingers.
- Don't taste and stir with the same spoon; use a clean spoon every time you taste the food.
- Don't put raw and cooked meat on the same shelf in the fridge. Store raw meat on a plate in wrapped packaging or in a sealed container, on the bottom shelf, so it can't touch or drip over other foods. Keep all perishable foods wrapped separately.
- Always transfer leftovers to a clean container and cover with a lid, cling film or foil. Leave until completely cold, then store in the fridge. Never put any warm food in the fridge. Cooked rice is particularly dangerous if left sitting in the warm kitchen for too long: cool it as quickly as possible (if plain-cooked, tip it in a colander and rinse it under the cold tap then drain thoroughly). Cover and store in the fridge as soon as possible.
- Never use the same cloth you used to wipe down a chopping board on which you have been cutting up meat, for instance, to wipe down your work surfaces – you will simply spread germs. Always wash your cloth well in hot, soapy water; I always use an anti-bacterial kitchen cleaner on all surfaces too.

- Use separate chopping boards for cutting up meat, fish, poultry, vegetables and bread.
- When reheating food, always make sure it is piping hot throughout, never just lukewarm. It is particularly important when microwaving that you leave the food to stand (*see* page 9) to allow the temperature to equalise through the food. Always do the 'knife test' (*see* below) to check food is hot all the way through. A plated meal is piping hot throughout if, after microwaving, the centre of the base of the plate feels piping hot. If not, microwave for a minute or two more.
- Don't re-freeze raw foods that have defrosted unless you cook them first (pastry is probably the only exception). Never reheat previously cooked food more than once.
- Always wipe out your cooker after use with a clean cloth wrung out in hot soapy water. If you leave food splattered on the insides not only will it discolour, become unsightly and difficult to remove but, when microwaving, the microwaves won't be able to differentiate between the real food to be cooked and the caked-on bits, so food will take longer to cook.

KNIFE TEST

When reheating made-up cooked dishes, such as a lasagne, insert a sharp knife blade into the centre after reheating. Wait 5 seconds then remove the knife and test the blade on the back of your hand. If should feel almost burning hot. If not, microwave for a few more minutes and test again.

A WELL-STOCKED STORECUPBOARD

Here's a list of all the items I've used in the book to help you get set up and ready to cook whenever you need to. This doesn't include fresh meat and vegetables, which I am assuming you will buy as you need.

DRY GOODS
Cornflakes/Weetabix
Digestive biscuits
Dried breadcrumbs
Haricot beans, dried (or use cans)
Medium egg noodles (preferably wholemeal)
Pasta: lasagne verdi sheets, pasta shapes, spaghetti and
    tagliatelle (preferably wholemeal)
Pearl barley
Puy lentils
Red lentils
Rice: basmati, risotto, paella, jasmine and short-grain
Rolled (porridge) oats
Straight-to-wok noodles
Stuffing mix

BAKING AIDS
Baking powder
Bicarbonate of soda
Cocoa powder

Cornflour

Dried fruits: apricots, cake mix, cranberries, dates, raisins, sultanas

Dried skimmed milk powder

Drinking chocolate powder

Easy-blend dried yeast

Flours: plain, self-raising, wholemeal, strong bread flours

Instant coffee granules

Nuts: almonds (ground and flaked), cashews, coconut (desiccated and flakes), peanuts, pinenuts, walnuts

Seeds: caraway, celery, cumin, fennel, black onion (nigella), pumpkin, sesame, sunflower

Sugar: caster (superfine), demerara, granulated, light and dark brown

HERBS AND SPICES

Basil, dried and fresh

Bay leaves

Bouquet garni sachets

Cajun spice blend

Chilli flakes, dried

Chilli powder and/or cayenne

Chinese five-spice powder

Chives, fresh and/or dried

Cinnamon, ground and sticks

Coriander, fresh and ground

Cumin, ground and seeds

Dill, fresh and/or dried

Garam masala

Garlic, whole cloves and/or a jar of purée (use about 1 tsp per garlic clove)

Ginger, ground, and fresh or a jar of grated
Harissa paste
Madras curry paste
Mint, dried
Mixed herbs, dried
Nutmeg, whole to grate is best
Oregano, dried
Paprika: sweet and smoked
Parsley, fresh
Pepper: black peppercorns in a mill and ground white
Rosemary, fresh and/or dried
Saffron strands
Sage, fresh and/or dried
Sambal oelek
Sea salt (fine and flakes)
Thyme, fresh and/or dried
Tumeric, ground
Vanilla extract, natural
Vanilla pods

JARS AND BOTTLES
Apple juice
Brown table sauce
Capers, pickled
Cranberry sauce
Gherkins, pickled
Honey – clear is best for cooking
Horseradish relish
Lemon and lime juices
Maple syrup

Marmite or other yeast extract
Mayonnaise
Mushroom ketchup
Mustard: ready-made English, Dijon and grainy
Oils: sunflower, olive and speciality ones like sesame and
    walnut for flavouring
Olives, black and green
Passata
Peanut butter
Plum jam
Redcurrant jelly
Soy sauce (choose naturally fermented)
Stock concentrate: beef, chicken and vegetable (or cubes)
Sundried tomatoes in oil
Tahini paste
Thai fish sauce
Thai red and green curry pastes
Tomato ketchup
Tomato purée
Vinegars: red or white wine, cider, white balsamic condiment,
    brown balsamic, rice
Worcestershire sauce

CANS
Carrots
Cream of mushroom soup
Custard
Fruit: pineapple, pears, peaches, raspberries
Pulses: chickpeas, red kidney beans, haricot beans, baked beans
    in tomato sauce, cannellini beans, lentils

Salmon

Sardines, in oil and tomato sauce

Sweetcorn

Tomatoes, chopped

Tuna (check the label for 'dolphin friendly')

FRIDGE AND FREEZER ESSENTIALS

Bread: baguettes, ciabatta, pitta breads, naans, sourdough, tortillas (flour and corn) etc., (store in the freezer and take out when required; some part-bakes are useful)

Butter

Cheeses: blue cheese, Camembert, Cheddar, Emmental, Parmesan, mozzarella, paneer, feta, halloumi

Cooking chorizo

Cream: double, single

Crème fraîche

Eggs, free-range: smallish (look for economy free-range eggs that vary in size in the box), medium and large

Frozen chopped onion (saves a lot of tears and effort!)

Ham

Pastry: shortcrust and filo

Peas, frozen

Milk: keep a carton in the freezer, too, so you won't run out; it takes ages to thaw and will need a good shake once defrosted

Yoghurt, plain (Greek-style is particularly good for cooking)

NOTES ON THE RECIPES

- All spoon measures are level: 1 tsp = 5ml; 1 tbsp = 15ml unless otherwise stated.
- Eggs are medium unless otherwise stated.
- Vegetables and fruit are medium-sized unless otherwise stated.
- Always wash fresh produce before use. Peel, core and seed if necessary.
- Seasoning and the use of strongly flavoured ingredients such as garlic or chillies is very much a matter of personal taste. Adjust to suit your own palate.
- Don't be afraid to cut a few corners: I don't mean just buying shortcrust pastry, but sometimes a pack of ready-grated cheese is no more expensive than buying it in a block, jars of garlic purée and grated fresh ginger are a real boon, and I wouldn't be without a bag of frozen, chopped onion. I simply use a good handful in place of 1 chopped onion – no more tears or effort!
- Always trim any excess fat or gristle from meat before use.
- All can and packet sizes are approximate as they vary from brand to brand. For example, if I specify to use a 400g can of chickpeas and yours is a 410g can – that's fine.
- Cooking times are approximate and should be used as a guide only. Always check food is piping hot and cooked through before serving.
- When recipes call for cream or crème fraîche, you should use full-fat varieties if it is added during cooking. You may

substitute low-fat varieties for cold dishes, stirring in at the last minute without reheating, or for decorating. If low-fat creams (including single cream) are brought to boiling point, they will curdle.

SOME USEFUL COOKING TIMES AND METHODS

These are all suggested and are a guide only. Always check food before the end of the cooking time – you can always add on more time but you cannot take it off once cooked!

Food	Quantity	Cooking method and time	Instructions
BEEF AND LAMB			
Burgers, fresh	400g (4)	MICROWAVE HIGH (100 per cent) 3–4 minutes.	Place on microwave-safe rack over a plate on turntable. Turn over halfway through cooking.
		GRILL HIGH (1) 15 minutes.	Place on the high rack, on metal tray if necessary, on turntable. Turn over halfway through cooking.
Casserole, basic	4 servings	COMBINATION: CONVECTION 160°C + LOW/WARM (10 per cent) 1 hour 30 minutes.	Place in a casserole dish with diced or sliced vegetables, stock and flavourings. Cover. Place on metal tray or low rack on turntable.
Mince	400–500g	MICROWAVE HIGH (100 per cent) 5–6 minutes then MEDIUM (50–60 per cent) for 15–20 minutes.	Place in microwave-safe dish. Place on turntable. Stir several times during initial cooking to break up the grains, then add stock and other flavourings and stir once or twice during cooking.

Food	Quantity	Cooking method and time	Instructions
Steaks	300g (2)–600g (4)	GRILL HIGH (1) 8–10 minutes (medium-rare), 15–20 minutes (well-done). Leave to stand 10 minutes.	Brush with oil. Place on high rack over metal tray, if necessary, on turntable. Turn over, and rearrange if necessary, halfway through cooking. Wrap in foil for standing.
Joints	Per 450g	COMBINATION: CONVECTION 180°C + MEDIUM-LOW/SIMMER (25–30 per cent), 13–15 minutes per 450g. Leave to stand for 10 minutes before carving.	Place in a roasting tin on the metal tray or low rack on the turntable. Turn over halfway through cooking. Cover with foil for standing.

CHICKEN

Food	Quantity	Cooking method and time	Instructions
Breasts	450g (4)	MICROWAVE MEDIUM (50–60 per cent) 12–14 minutes.	Place in a microwave-safe dish. Season and add a little stock. Cover. Place on turntable. Turn over halfway through cooking.
		GRILL HIGH (1) 30 minutes.	For breasts with skin on or if wrapped in bacon. Brush with oil. Season. Place on the high rack over the metal tray or a plate on turntable. Turn halfway through cooking.

Food	Quantity	Cooking method and time	Instructions
Legs or thighs	900g (8)	MICROWAVE MEDIUM (50–60 per cent) 12–14 minutes.	Brush with soy sauce or dust with paprika or other flavourings/ browning agents (see page 8). Place on a microwave-safe rack or plate on turntable. Turn over halfway through cooking.
		CONVECTION 220°C 25–30 minutes.	Place in a roasting tin, on the metal tray if necessary, on turntable. Brush with oil and season as desired.
Whole	Per 450g	MICROWAVE MEDIUM-HIGH (70 per cent) 8 minutes per 450g, then leave to stand for 30 minutes.	Stuff the neck end, if liked, or put fresh herbs or half an onion in the body cavity. Weigh and calculate cooking time. Brush with a browning agent, if liked (see page 8) or use a roaster bag (see page 21). Start upside down in a microwave-safe dish on turntable. Turn halfway through cooking. After cooking, cover with foil for standing time.
		COMBINATION: CONVECTION 190°C + MEDIUM-LOW/SIMMER (25–30 per cent) 13–15 minutes per 450g.	Rub with oil, sprinkle with salt and place upside down in a roasting tin. Place on the metal tray or low rack on turntable. Turn over halfway

Food	Quantity	Cooking method and time	Instructions
EGGS			
Baked	Per egg	MICROWAVE HIGH (100 per cent) 15 seconds per egg, leave to stand 1 minute then MICROWAVE HIGH 20 seconds per egg.	Break egg into buttered ramekin. Prick yolk twice with cocktail stick. Add 1 tsp double cream and seasoning. Arrange ramekins in a circle on turntable.
Poached	Per egg	MICROWAVE HIGH (100 per cent) 30 seconds first egg, 20–30 seconds for each additional one (depending how you like them cooked). Leave to stand for 1 minute to complete cooking.	Put 2cm boiling water in a ramekin dish. Break in egg. Prick yolk twice with cocktail stick. If cooking several eggs, arrange ramekins in a circle on turntable.
Scrambled	Per egg	MICROWAVE HIGH (100 per cent) 30 seconds per egg. Leave to stand for 1 minute to complete cooking.	Suitable for up to 8 eggs. Beat in a bowl with 1 tbsp milk per egg. Add a knob of butter. Season. Place on turntable. Stir several times during cooking. Stop cooking while still slightly runny.

Food	Quantity	Cooking method and time	Instructions
FISH			
Baked	Per 450g	MICROWAVE HIGH (100 per cent) 4–6 minutes per 450g.	Calculate total weight of fish. Slash the cleaned fish on each side in several places with a sharp knife. Lay head to tail in a shallow dish. Dot with a little butter and sprinkle with lemon juice or add 2 tbsp water, stock or wine per fish. Cover. Place on turntable. Turn after 3 minutes.
		GRILL MEDIUM (2) 12–15 minutes, depending on size.	Slash and dot with butter as above. Place on the metal tray, greased, or a baking tray on high rack on turntable. Turn halfway through cooking.
Fillets	4 (approx. 450g)	MICROWAVE HIGH (100 per cent) 3–5 minutes (depending on thickness). Leave to stand 2 minutes to finish cooking.	Place in a single layer in a shallow microwave-safe dish. Add 60ml milk or water. Cover. Place on turntable. The cooking liquid can be used to make an accompanying sauce.
		GRILL HIGH (1) 8–12 minutes (depending on thickness).	Place skin side up on the metal tray, greased, or a baking tray, on high rack on turntable. If thick, turn halfway through cooking.

Food	Quantity	Cooking method and time	Instructions
FRUIT			
Apples, baked	Per good-sized cooking apple	MICROWAVE HIGH (100 per cent) 2 minutes per apple (depending on size) or until tender but still holding its shape.	Core but leave whole then cut a line round the skin halfway down each apple. Stand in a shallow microwave-safe dish. Fill centres with dried fruit and/or nuts and add a spoonful of syrup or honey over each. Cover.
Pears, poached	450g	MICROWAVE HIGH (100 per cent) 3–8 minutes depending on size and ripeness.	Peel but leave whole. Place in a microwave-safe dish. Add 300ml apple juice or half wine half apple juice, and a cinnamon stick or star anise, if liked. Cover.
Plums, stewed	450g	MICROWAVE HIGH (100 per cent) 3–5 minutes, depending on ripeness. Cook a little longer if you like your fruit pulpy.	Halve and stone. Arrange in a shallow dish. Sprinkle with sugar add 30ml water. Cover.
Rhubarb, stewed	450g	MICROWAVE HIGH (100 per cent) 6–8 minutes (depending on thickness).	Trim and cut into short lengths. Only half fill a dish and spread evenly. Add a good sprinkling of sugar and grated ginger or orange zest, if liked (or try lavender sugar). Add 2 tbsp water. Cover.

Food	Quantity	Cooking method and time	Instructions
PASTA			
Egg noodles	4 nests/ slabs	MICROWAVE HIGH (100 per cent) 4 minutes	Place in a large dish and cover with boiling water (not more than ⅓ full to allow for bubbling up). Stir once halfway through cooking.
Spaghetti/ tagliatelle	225g	MICROWAVE HIGH (100 per cent) 8–11 minutes (depending on brand and if plain or wholemeal). Leave to stand 5 minutes, then drain.	Don't cook more than 450g at one time. Place in a large dish and add at least 1.5 litres boiling water and a pinch of salt. Stir once or twice during cooking. Cover with foil for standing.
Shapes	225g	MICROWAVE HIGH (100 per cent) 10–11 minutes (depending on brand and if plain or wholemeal). Leave to stand 5 minutes, then drain.	Place in a large dish and add at least 1.5 litres boiling water and a pinch of salt. Stir once or twice during cooking. Don't cook more than 500g at one time. Cover with foil for standing.
PORK AND BACON			
Bacon rashers	Per rasher	MICROWAVE HIGH (100 per cent) 45 seconds per rasher.	Lay on a microwave-safe rack over a plate on the turntable. Place a sheet of kitchen paper over to prevent splattering.
		GRILL HIGH (1) 10 minutes.	Lay on the high rack over the metal tray, if necessary, on turntable. Turn over halfway through cooking.

Food	Quantity	Cooking method and time	Instructions
Casserole, basic	4 servings	COMBINATION: CONVECTION 160°C + LOW/WARM (10 per cent) 1 hour 30 minutes.	Place in a casserole with diced or sliced vegetables, stock and flavourings. Cover. Place on metal tray or low rack on turntable.
Chops/steaks	450g	GRILL HIGH (1) 15–20 minutes. Leave to stand 10 minutes.	Place on the high rack, on the metal tray if necessary, on the turntable. Turn over halfway through. Wrap in foil for standing.
Joints	Per 450g	COMBINATION: CONVECTION 170°C + MEDIUM-LOW/SIMMER (25–30 per cent) 18–20 minutes per 450g. Leave to stand 30 minutes.	Place in a roasting tin on the metal tray or low rack on turntable. Score the skin deeply and rub with salt if there is crackling, and do not turn. If no crackling, turn over halfway through cooking. Wrap in foil for standing.
Sausages	4–8	GRILL HIGH (1) 15–20 minutes.	Place on the high rack, over the metal tray if necessary, on the turntable. Turn over and rearrange two or three times during cooking.
Tenderloin	Per 450g	COMBINATION: 190°C + LOW/WARM (10 per cent) 20–25 minutes per 450g. Leave to stand for 20 minutes.	Partially split, stuff, tie up if liked, then weigh. Place, coiled round if necessary, in a roasting tin on the metal tray or low rack on turntable. Rub all over with oil and season. Wrap in foil for standing.

Food	Quantity	Cooking method and time	Instructions
PULSES			
Chickpeas	225g	HIGH (100 per cent) 10 minutes MEDIUM-LOW/ SIMMER (25–30 per cent) 40–50 minutes or until tender. Leave to stand for 5 minutes.	Soak in plenty of cold water for several hours or overnight. Drain, place in a large microwave-safe bowl. Cover with plenty of boiling water. Add more, if necessary during cooking. After cooking, season then cover with foil for standing. Drain if necessary.
Lentils, brown	225g	HIGH (100 per cent) 25–30 minutes or until tender. Leave to stand for 5 minutes.	No need to soak, just wash well. Place in a large microwave-safe bowl. Cover with plenty of boiling water. Season after cooking and cover with foil for standing. Drain if necessary.
Lentils, red	225g	HIGH (100 per cent) 20 minutes or until soft. Leave to stand for 2 minutes.	No need to soak. Place in a large microwave-safe bowl. Add 600ml boiling water. Cover with a lid or plate. Season after cooking, then re-cover for standing.
Red kidney beans	225g	HIGH (100 per cent) 15 minutes MEDIUM-LOW/ SIMMER (25–30 per cent) 40 minutes or until soft. Leave to stand for 5 minutes.	Soak in cold water for several hours or overnight. Drain. Place in a large microwave-safe bowl. Cover with plenty of boiling water. Season after cooking. Cover with foil for standing. Drain if necessary.

Food	Quantity	Cooking method and time	Instructions
RICE			
Basmati	250g	MICROWAVE MEDIUM (50–60 per cent) 10–15 minutes. Cover with foil and leave to stand for at least 5 minutes until the liquid is absorbed.	Wash rice. Place in a large microwave-safe bowl. Add 600ml boiling water and a pinch of salt (it should be no more than ⅓ full). Stir. Cover with a lid or plate. Fluff up with a fork before serving.
Brown, long-grain	250g	MICROWAVE MEDIUM (50–60 per cent) 20–25 minutes. Cover with foil and leave to stand for at least 5 minutes until the liquid is absorbed.	Wash rice. Place in a large microwave-safe bowl. Add 600ml boiling water and a pinch of salt (it should be no more than ⅓ full). Stir. Cover with a lid or plate. Fluff up with a fork before serving.
Jasmine	250g	MICROWAVE HIGH (100 per cent) 12 minutes. Cover with foil and leave to stand for 10 minutes or until liquid is absorbed and the rice is sticky.	Place in a large microwave-safe bowl with 750ml boiling water and a pinch of salt (it should be no more than ⅓ full). Cover with a lid or plate. Stir once after cooking and again before serving.
Round/ short-grain rice for rice pudding (for risotto *see* page 141)	50g	MICROWAVE HIGH (100 per cent) 5 minutes, then MEDIUM-LOW/ SIMMER (25–30 per cent) 35 minutes. To brown when cooked (optional) GRILL HIGH (1) 5–10 minutes.	Mix rice with 450ml milk and 2 tbsp sugar in a fairly shallow microwave-safe dish. Place on turntable. When cooked, leave to stand for 10 minutes or for brown skin, place on high rack on metal tray, if necessary, on turntable.

Food	Quantity	Cooking method and time	Instructions
VEGETABLES			
Beans, green/ runner	450g	MICROWAVE HIGH (100 per cent) 6–7 minutes. Leave to stand for 4 minutes.	String and diagonally slice runners or top and tail green beans. Put in an even layer in a shallow microwave-safe dish. Add 6 tbsp water. Cover with a lid or plate. Place on turntable. Drain after standing.
Broccoli	450g	MICROWAVE HIGH (100 per cent) 8 minutes. Leave to stand for 3 minutes.	Cut into even-sized florets. Arrange, heads towards the centre, in a shallow microwave-safe dish. Add 6 tbsp water. Cover with a lid or plate. Place on turntable. Drain after standing.
Cabbage	450g	MICROWAVE HIGH (100 per cent) 6–9 minutes depending on type. Leave to stand for 3 minutes.	Trim thick stalks then shred. Put in an even layer in a shallow microwave-safe dish. Add 6 tbsp water. Cover with a lid or plate. Place on turntable. Drain after standing.
Carrots	450g	MICROWAVE HIGH (100 per cent) 7–9 minutes depending on size of pieces. Leave to stand for 3 minutes.	Scrub or scrape and slice or cut into matchsticks. Put in an even layer in a shallow microwave-safe dish. Add 6 tbsp water. Cover with a lid or plate. Place on turntable. Drain after standing.

Food	Quantity	Cooking method and time	Instructions
Cauliflower: Steamed	1 medium	MICROWAVE HIGH (100 per cent) 10–12 minutes. Leave to stand for 4 minutes.	Separate into even-sized florets, discarding thick stump. Arrange, heads to the centre of a shallow microwave-safe dish. Trim and add some of the green, if liked. Add 6 tbsp water. Cover with a lid or plate. Place on the turntable. Drain after standing.
Cauliflower: Baked in sauce	1 medium	MICROWAVE HIGH (100 per cent) 10–12 minutes then COMBINATION: 220°C + LOW/WARM (10 per cent) 12–15 minutes or until browning on top.	Cook as above but for 8 minutes until nearly tender. Drain. Cover with 1 quantity cheese sauce (see page 187). Sprinkle with crushed cornflakes or bran flakes, if liked. Sprinkle with extra grated Cheddar. Place on metal tray or low rack on turntable.
Peas	450g	MICROWAVE HIGH (100 per cent) 5–6 minutes. Leave to stand 2 minutes.	Place fresh or frozen peas in a shallow microwave-safe dish. Add 6 tbsp water. Cover and place on the turntable. Drain after standing. Alternatively, to cook a whole bag of frozen peas. Make a slit in the bag, place on the turntable. Cook as before, flexing and shaking the bag from time to time. Drain off any water.

Food	Quantity	Cooking method and time	Instructions
Potatoes: Boiled	450g	MICROWAVE HIGH (100 per cent) 7–9 minutes, depending on size. Leave to stand for 3 minutes.	Scrub or peel and cut into even-sized pieces if large. Add 6 tbsp water. Cover with a lid or plate. Drain after standing.
Potatoes: Jacket	4 large	MICROWAVE HIGH (100 per cent) 13 minutes. Leave to stand for 4 minutes. COMBINATION: CONVECTION 220°C + MEDIUM-LOW/ SIMMER (25–30 per cent) 25 minutes.	Scrub and prick all over with a fork. Wrap each in kitchen paper. Arrange around turntable. Wrap in foil for standing time. Scrub and prick as before. Place apart on the metal tray or low rack on the turntable.
Roast	450g	MICROWAVE HIGH (100 per cent) 4 minutes then COMBINATION: CONVECTION 220°C + LOW/WARM (10 per cent) 25 minutes.	Peel and cut into even-sized chunks. Place in a microwave-safe dish with 6 tbsp water. Cover, place on the turntable. Drain. Place in a baking tin with 45ml olive or sunflower oil. Toss gently. Place on the metal tray or low rack on turntable. Turn over halfway through cooking.

BREAKFASTS

When you want something truly delicious to start your day, why not let your combination cooker do the work for you? The dish you use to cook your scrambled eggs or porridge won't be nearly as hard to clean as a saucepan heated on the hob. Foods like mushrooms retain all their flavour and goodness, and as for toasted muesli, well you can make it in half the time it would take to bake conventionally – and then pop it in a sealed container for scrumptious ultra-healthy breakfasts for days to come.

SCRAMBLED EGGS
AND PORTOBELLO MUSHROOMS

You can, of course, make plain scrambled eggs and serve on buttered toast. Try, too, throwing in a couple of chopped tomatoes or diced pimientos from a jar before you leave the scrambled eggs to stand.

Serves 4

4 very large portobello mushrooms
1 tbsp sunflower oil
Salt and freshly ground black pepper
6 large eggs
4 tbsp milk
A large knob of butter
1 tbsp double cream (optional)
1 tbsp chopped fresh parsley

To serve
Buttered toast or hot rolls

1 Peel the mushrooms and cut off the stalks. Brush all over the white sides with the oil and season with very little salt and plenty of pepper. Brush the metal tray or a baking sheet, with oil, too, and place the mushrooms, gill sides down, on it. Place the tray on the high rack on the turntable.

2 GRILL on MEDIUM (2) for 4 minutes, turn over and grill for a further 4 minutes or until just tender but still with some texture. Remove from the oven and wrap in foil to keep warm.

3 Meanwhile, beat the eggs in a microwave-safe bowl with the milk and some seasoning. Add the knob of butter.

4 MICROWAVE on the turntable on HIGH (100 per cent) for 3 minutes. Remove from the oven and stir with a fork after every minute. When cooked, stir again with the fork to scramble the eggs, stir in the cream, if using, and leave to stand for 2 minutes to finish setting.

5 Place the mushrooms on warm plates and spoon the egg on top. Sprinkle with chopped fresh parsley and serve with hot toast or rolls.

EGGS ROYALE

These are English muffins, topped with smoked salmon, poached eggs and Hollandaise sauce. I use smoked salmon trimmings, which you can buy fairly cheaply (compared with sliced smoked salmon), but you could, of course, use whole slices instead. For the traditional Eggs Benedict, substitute slices of ham for the fish.

Serves 4

1 quantity Hollandaise sauce (*see* page 186)
2 English muffins, halved
Butter for spreading
Boiling water
4 eggs
120g smoked salmon trimmings
Cayenne pepper

1   Make the Hollandaise sauce. Cover with a circle of wet baking paper and stand it in a larger bowl of hot but not boiling water to keep warm.

2   Put the muffin halves, cut sides up, on the high rack over the metal plate, if necessary, on the turntable. GRILL on HIGH (1) for 3–4 minutes or until toasted. Spread with butter and wrap in foil to keep warm.

3   Fill 4 ramekins with about 2cm boiling water. Break an egg into each and prick the yolks twice with a cocktail stick. MICROWAVE on HIGH (100 per cent) for 1½–2 minutes or until cooked to your liking. Leave to stand for 1 minute.

4 Meanwhile put the muffin halves on warm plates and top with the smoked salmon trimmings, pressing them down well to flatten.

5 Carefully tip an egg at a time out of the dishes into a draining spoon (over the sink or a bowl to catch the water) and place one egg on top of each muffin. Stir the Hollandaise and spoon over, dust with a little cayenne and serve straight away.

BEAN AND POTATO TORTILLA

If you have some cooked leftover potatoes, cut them into fairly thin slices or small pieces, toss in the oil with the spring onions and microwave on HIGH for 30 seconds only to heat, before adding the remaining ingredients. This is also good cold, cut into wedges to put in lunchboxes.

Serves 4

2 potatoes, scrubbed and thinly sliced
2 spring onions, trimmed and finely chopped
2 tbsp olive oil
400g can baked beans in tomato sauce
Salt and freshly ground black pepper
6 eggs

1 Toss the potatoes and spring onions in the oil in a 23cm microwave-safe, ovenproof flan dish. Spread out evenly in the dish. Cover with cling film rolled back slightly at one edge to allow steam to escape. Place on the turntable. MICROWAVE on HIGH (100 per cent) for 4 minutes, stirring and turning once until tender.
2 Stir in the baked beans and a little salt and some black pepper. Beat the eggs with just a little more salt and pepper and pour into the dish. Stir gently to distribute evenly.
3 Place on the metal tray or low rack on the turntable and cook on COMBINATION: CONVECTION 190°C + MEDIUM (50–60 per cent) for 15 minutes until set and golden on top. Leave to cool slightly, then serve warm cut into wedges.

QUICK OMELETTE BAPS

These are also delicious served cold for breakfast on the run, or even for lunch with some shredded lettuce, sliced tomato, and mayonnaise instead of ketchup or brown sauce.

Serves 4

Large knob of butter, plus extra for spreading
4 eggs
Salt and freshly ground black pepper
1 tbsp fresh snipped or 1½ tsp dried chives
4 soft wholegrain baps, split into halves
Tomato ketchup or brown sauce (optional)

1 Put the butter in a 20cm microwave-safe flan dish. Cover the dish loosely with kitchen paper (to prevent splattering) and MICROWAVE on HIGH (100 per cent) for 50 seconds to melt.

2 Beat the eggs with a little salt and pepper and add the chives. Pour into the dish. MICROWAVE on HIGH for 2 minutes, stirring gently after 1 minute. Remove from the oven, cover the dish with foil and leave to stand while you prepare the bread rolls.

3 Put the halved rolls, cut sides up, on the high rack on the metal tray, if necessary, on the turntable. GRILL on HIGH (1) for 3 minutes until toasted on the one side. Spread with butter.

4 Spread the bottom halves of the rolls with tomato ketchup or brown sauce, if using, and then top each with a quarter of the omelette. Add the bread roll 'lids' and serve.

HOMEMADE BAKED BEANS IN TOMATO SAUCE

These are packed with goodness and utterly delicious. You can speed things up considerably by using two 400g cans haricot beans, drained, and starting the recipe at step 3. The baked beans are best made in advance and kept in the fridge, as not only does the flavour improve but it would be too much of an effort to make them fresh in the morning for breakfast! They will keep for several days.

Serves 4

200g dried haricot beans
600ml boiling water
1 onion, finely chopped
1 celery stick, finely chopped
1 tbsp sunflower oil
90g chorizo or pancetta, finely diced
450ml passata
1 tbsp clear honey
1 large bay leaf
½ tsp smoked paprika if using pancetta (optional)
1 tbsp mushroom ketchup
1 large bay leaf
Salt and freshly ground black pepper

To serve
Buttered wholegrain or sourdough toast

1   Soak the beans in plenty of cold water for several hours or overnight. Drain and place in a large microwave-safe bowl. Cover with the boiling water. Place on the turntable and microwave on HIGH (100 per cent) for 10 minutes to remove toxins, then MICROWAVE on MEDIUM-LOW/SIMMER (30 per cent) for 45–50 minutes or until really soft (make sure they are because they won't soften any more once you add the remaining ingredients). Cover with foil or a lid and leave to stand while preparing the remaining ingredients.

2   Mix the onion, celery, oil and chorizo in a large microwave-safe, ovenproof casserole. Place on the turntable and MICROWAVE on HIGH for 3 minutes to soften the vegetables and let the fat run from the sausage.

3   Stir in the remaining ingredients, including the beans together with any remaining cooking water, and season well. Cover and cook on COMBINATION: CONVECTION 180°C + MEDIUM-LOW/SIMMER (25–30 per cent) for 30 minutes until the beans are bathed in a rich sauce. Stir in a little boiling water if too dry. Leave to stand for 5 minutes. Discard the bay leaf, taste and re-season if necessary. Serve on buttered wholegrain or sourdough toast.

SMOKED HADDOCK, FETA AND SPINACH KEDGEREE

A traditional kedgeree does not include feta or spinach like this one, simply the fish, parsley and, usually, some cooked peas. Feel free to omit if you prefer a simpler breakfast or brunch.

Serves 4

250g basmati rice
650ml boiling water
Salt and freshly ground black pepper
1 shallot, very finely chopped
75g frozen peas
1 bay leaf
100g spinach, shredded
300g undyed smoked haddock fillet, skinned
120ml milk
2 tbsp chopped fresh parsley
A good grating of fresh nutmeg
A splash of Thai fish sauce (optional)
100g feta cheese, crumbled
2 hard-boiled eggs, quartered (optional)

1   Wash the rice and put in a large bowl with the boiling water, a pinch of salt and the shallot. Stir. Place on the turntable and MICROWAVE on HIGH (100 per cent) for 10 minutes. Stir, add the peas and bay leaf and MICROWAVE on HIGH for a further 5 minutes. Remove from the oven, stir in the spinach, cover with foil to keep hot and leave to stand while preparing the rest of the dish.

2 Put the fish and milk in a shallow dish. MICROWAVE on HIGH for 3 minutes. Leave to stand for 1 minute, then flake with a fork into chunky pieces.

3 Tip into the rice and gently stir through the spinach mixture, half the parsley and plenty of pepper. Add a good grating of nutmeg and a splash of Thai fish sauce, if liked. MICROWAVE on HIGH for 1 minute to reheat, if necessary.

4 Spoon into shallow bowls and crumble the feta on top. Top each with two quarters of hard-boiled egg, if using, and serve straight away.

TOASTED MAPLE MUESLI WITH CRANBERRIES

This is not a sickly sweet, hard granola but a moreish, packed-with-goodness toasted muesli with just a hint of background sweetness from the small amount of maple syrup used in the toasting. For a hot breakfast, mix a portion in a bowl with cold milk, then microwave on HIGH for 1 minute and serve topped with fresh blueberries. If you like a crunchier texture, add the fruit before baking.

Makes about 8 servings

200g rolled oats
100g oat bran
50g sunflower seeds
50g pumpkin seeds
50g sesame seeds
50g unsweetened large coconut flakes
½ tsp ground cinnamon
2 tbsp sunflower or rapeseed oil
2 tbsp apple juice
2 tbsp maple syrup or clear honey
50g dried cranberries
50g raisins

To serve
Milk or plain yoghurt

1 Mix the oats, bran, seeds and coconut and cinnamon together in large bowl.

2 Mix the oil, apple juice and maple syrup together until the syrup has dissolved. Add to the oat mixture and mix well until thoroughly combined.

3 Spread out evenly on the metal tray or a non-stick baking sheet that will fit the turntable and place on the turntable in the oven.

4 Cook on COMBINATION: CONVECTION 160°C + LOW/WARM (10 per cent) for 15 minutes, turning and stirring every 5 minutes, until a lot of the oats and coconut are toasted but not too brown. Remove from the oven and stir in the fruit. Leave to cool. Store in an airtight container and serve with milk or plain yoghurt.

TEACUP PORRIDGE

This makes a nice, creamy porridge. If you like yours a bit thicker, use 1½ teacups each of milk and water. You can also use all milk or all water, if you prefer a lighter or richer breakfast.

Serves 4—6

2 teacupfuls rolled oats
Pinch of salt
2 teacupfuls milk
2 teacupfuls water

To serve
Milk and honey

1 Mix the porridge in a large bowl with the salt, milk and water.
2 MICROWAVE on HIGH (100 per cent) on the turntable 8–9 minutes until thick and creamy, stirring once or twice.
3 Serve with milk and honey.

VARIATION
With apple and cinnamon
Prepare as above, but stir in a large peeled, cored and diced eating apple, 1 teaspoon ground cinnamon and 1 tbsp clear honey before you start cooking. Serve each portion sprinkled with a spoonful of chopped toasted mixed nuts.

SOUPS, SNACKS
AND LIGHT MEALS

Your combination cooker will really come into its own for making quick meals and snacks. Soups are great because the kitchen doesn't get steamed-up in the way it does when a pot is left simmering away on the hob. It's easy to make individual snacks, too – particularly on the grill, rather than heating the huge element in a conventional cooker. You can speed up the cooking of so many things, from pizzas to noodle dishes, and knock up extra-special snacks and light meals in no time at all.

SWEET POTATO, CARROT AND CREAM CHEESE SOUP

Rich and satisfying, this soup is wonderful on a cold winter's day. The cheese in it adds protein, too. Served with some crusty bread and perhaps some fruit afterwards, it makes a complete light lunch or supper.

Serves 4

1 onion, chopped
A knob of butter
1 tsp ground cumin
1 sweet potato (about 350g), peeled and cut into chunks
2 carrots, peeled and sliced
1 potato, peeled and cut into small chunks
750ml vegetable stock
150ml milk
4 tbsp soft white garlic and herb cheese
2 tbsp chopped fresh coriander

1   Put the onion, butter and cumin in a large microwave-safe bowl and MICROWAVE on HIGH (100 per cent) for 2 minutes. Add the prepared vegetables and stock. Cover the bowl with a plate or cling film rolled back slightly at one edge and MICROWAVE on HIGH for 20 minutes until the vegetables are really tender.

2   Blitz with a hand blender or tip into a blender goblet and purée. Add the milk, cheese and half the coriander and purée again. Season to taste and serve hot garnished with the remaining chopped fresh coriander.

ONION, CABBAGE AND SAUSAGE SOUP WITH CHEESE AND MUSTARD TOASTS

There is nothing more sustaining on a cold winter's day – or a dark, bleak one in autumn or spring, for that matter – than a bowl of really hearty soup, packed with flavour. This one fits the bill perfectly.

Serves 4

A good knob of butter
2 large onions, halved and thinly sliced
¼ small white cabbage, finely shredded
1 smoked pork sausage ring, cut into 5mm slices
1 bay leaf
1 litre hot beef or chicken stock
Salt and freshly ground black pepper
1 tbsp soy sauce
2 tbsp chopped fresh parsley
4 diagonally cut slices of baguette
2 teaspoons Dijon mustard
50g grated Cheddar or other melting cheese

1   Put the butter, onions and cabbage in a large microwave-safe bowl on the turntable and MICROWAVE on HIGH (100 per cent) for 5 minutes, stirring occasionally until softening.

2   Add the sausage, bay leaf, stock, just a pinch of salt, a good grinding of pepper and the soy sauce. Cover the bowl with a plate or cling film rolled back slightly at one edge and MICROWAVE on HIGH for 20 minutes. Remove from the oven add the parsley, cover with foil and leave to stand.

3   Place the baguette slices on the high rack over the metal tray, if necessary, on the turntable and GRILL on HIGH (1) for 3 minutes until golden. Turn the bread over. Mix the mustard with the cheese and spread on the bread. Grill again for 2–3 minutes or until melted and bubbling.

4   Ladle the soup into warm bowls, discarding the bay leaf, and float a cheese and mustard toast in each bowl before serving.

CREAM OF TOMATO AND ROASTED RED PEPPER SOUP WITH FRESH TOMATO SALSA

I find you really need the tiny hit of sugar or honey to bring out the full flavour of the tomatoes in this vibrant soup, but you can omit if you prefer. The pepper has a delicious smoky flavour when roasted first, but if time is short you can simply chop it and soften it with the onion at step 2. Just cook them for an extra minute or two.

Serve 4

1 red pepper
1 tbsp sunflower oil
1 shallot, chopped
1 garlic clove, crushed
400g can chopped tomatoes
600ml hot vegetable stock
1 bouquet garni sachet
2 tbsp tomato purée
1 tsp caster sugar or clear honey
Salt and freshly ground black pepper
120ml double cream

For the salsa
2 ripe tomatoes, seeded and finely chopped
1 tbsp chopped fresh basil

1 Put the red pepper on the high rack on the metal tray, if necessary, on the turntable. GRILL on HIGH (1) for 5 minutes. Turn it over and grill for a further 5 minutes until blackened in places. Put the pepper in a plastic bag and leave to cool.

2 Put the oil, shallot and garlic in a large microwave-safe bowl. Stir well. Place in the oven on the turntable and MICROWAVE on HIGH (100 per cent) for 2 minutes until softened.

3 Stir in the canned tomatoes, stock, bouquet garni, tomato purée, sugar and some salt and pepper. MICROWAVE on HIGH for a further 3 minutes, stirring once.

4 Meanwhile, when the pepper is cool enough to handle, scrape off the charred skin, halve, remove the stalk and seeds and roughly chop the flesh. Add most to the soup, reserving a small spoonful to add to the salsa. MICROWAVE on HIGH for a further 5 minutes. Discard the bouquet garni, squeezing it well against the sides of the bowl to extract maximum flavour. Purée the soup in a blender or food processor.

5 Return the soup to the bowl and stir in all but 2 tbsp of the cream. Taste and re-season as necessary. Microwave for a further minute to reheat but do not allow to boil.

6 Meanwhile, make the salsa. Finely chop the reserved chopped pepper and mix with the chopped fresh tomato and basil then season to taste. Ladle the soup into warm bowls. Add a swirl of the remaining cream to each and top with a spoonful of the salsa.

CRISPY BEEF TACOS

To make enough for 12 tacos (the amount you get in a pack), divide the meat more thinly and top with a salsa of some finely diced avocado, tomato, onion and some extra chopped fresh coriander, moistened with a squeeze of lemon or lime juice.

Serves 4

1 onion, finely chopped
1 garlic clove, crushed
1 green pepper, seeded and finely chopped
1 tbsp sunflower oil
225g lean minced beef
½ tsp dried chilli flakes (or to taste)
½ tsp ground cumin
½ tsp dried oregano
120ml passata or beef stock
1 tbsp tomato purée
½ tsp caster sugar
Salt and freshly ground black pepper
1 tbsp chopped fresh coriander (optional)
8 crispy tacos
A large handful shredded lettuce
A large handful grated Cheddar cheese
120ml soured cream or crème fraîche

1   Mix the onion, garlic and green pepper with the oil in a large microwave-safe bowl. Place in the oven on the turntable and MICROWAVE on HIGH (100 per cent) for 2 minutes, stirring once until softened.

2   Stir in the minced beef and MICROWAVE on HIGH for 3 minutes, stirring and breaking up every minute until browned and all the grains are separate. Stir in the chilli flakes, cumin and oregano and microwave for 30 seconds.

3   Add the passata, tomato purée, sugar and some salt and pepper. MICROWAVE on HIGH for a further 10 minutes until rich and thick. Remove from the oven, stir in the coriander, if using, and cover with foil to keep warm.

4   Arrange the taco shells open sides down on the metal tray or low rack on the turntable. GRILL on MEDIUM (2) for 3 minutes.

5   Spoon the hot beef mixture into the taco shells, top each with some shredded lettuce, cheese and a dollop of soured cream or crème fraîche and serve straight away.

FAST CHEESE AND TOMATO NOODLES

If you only have the dried egg noodles, simply cook them in the microwave in boiling water on HIGH (100 per cent) for 4 minutes before making the sauce. Serve with a crisp salad for a complete meal, doubling the quantity for big appetites.

Serves 4

300g fresh egg or straight-to-wok medium noodles
200ml passata
1 tbsp tomato purée
½ tsp caster sugar
Salt and freshly ground black pepper
½ tsp dried basil
75g strong Cheddar cheese, grated

To garnish
Grated Parmesan or extra Cheddar

1   If using fresh noodles, put them in a large bowl and cover with boiling water. Place on the turntable and MICROWAVE on HIGH (100 per cent) for 3 minutes. Drain in a colander.
2   In the same bowl, mix the passata and tomato purée until well blended then stir in the sugar, some salt and pepper and the basil. MICROWAVE on HIGH for 3 minutes, stirring once.
3   Add the cooked fresh noodles, or if using straight-to-wok noodles, carefully crumble them into the sauce to separate the strands. Add the Cheddar and toss well. MICROWAVE on HIGH for a further 2 minutes then serve with grated Parmesan or more Cheddar to sprinkle over.

BAKED CAMEMBERT WITH CRUDITÉS

Ideally the Camembert should be just ripe, so it gives slightly when pressed, but should not smell of ammonia. If you can't get one in a wooden box, transfer the cheese to a small round dish that will hold it snugly before cooking.

Serves 4—6

For the crudités
2 large carrots, cut into thirds widthways, then in batons
2 celery sticks, cut into quarters, then in batons
1 green and 1 red pepper, halved, seeded and cut into strips
¼ cucumber, halved widthways and cut into batons

For the Camembert
1 wheel of Camembert in a wooden box
1 garlic clove, halved
2 tsp dry white wine
½ tsp dried mixed herbs

To serve
Crusty baguette

1   First prepare the crudités, arrange on a platter, cover and chill until needed.

2   Unwrap the Camembert, rub it all over with the garlic then put it back in its box without the wrapper.

3   Place on the metal tray or a baking sheet that will fit the turntable. Pierce holes in the cheese with a skewer and drizzle over the white wine. Sprinkle with the herbs.

4   Cook on COMBINATION: CONVECTION 220°C + LOW/WARM (10 per cent) for 7 minutes until the cheese is melting and bubbling. Serve straight away in the box with the crudités and chunks of crusty baguette for dipping.

EXOTIC MUSHROOM AND EGG PIZZA

It's important, I find, to cook the base before adding the topping to ensure the dough is properly cooked through before the cheese browns too much. Here, I've given you a choice of two of my favourite toppings, but you could, of course, use just cheese and tomato or add pepperoni, ham, anchovies, peppers, olives – or anything you fancy.

Serves 4

225g strong bread flour
Salt and freshly ground black pepper
½ tsp caster sugar
2 tsp fast-action dried yeast
Olive oil
125ml warm water
1 onion, finely chopped
1 garlic clove, crushed
200g mixed exotic mushrooms (chanterelle, oyster, chestnut, eryngii, shiitake etc.), wiped and sliced into smaller pieces if large
1 tsp fresh thyme
4 tbsp crème fraîche
4 tbsp white soft cheese with garlic and herbs
115g mozzarella, grated
4 smallish eggs (don't use large ones or the white won't set before the yolks harden)

1   Mix the flour with ½ tsp salt, the sugar and yeast. Add 1 tbsp olive oil and enough of the water to form a soft but not too sticky dough.

2   Knead gently on a lightly floured surface for 5 minutes. Dust the surface with cornmeal or a little more flour and roll out to a 30cm round.

3   Place on the metal tray (if your oven has one), oiled, or on a large pizza plate. Set aside.

4   Put 1 tbsp olive oil in a microwave-safe dish. Add the onion and garlic. Stir, then place on the turntable and MICROWAVE on HIGH (100 per cent) for 3 minutes until softened. Add the mushrooms and thyme and stir. MICROWAVE on HIGH for a further 2 minutes then season with a little salt and pepper.

5   Put the pizza base in the oven on the turntable or low rack and cook on COMBINATION: CONVECTION 220°C + LOW/WARM (10 per cent) for 6 minutes until puffing up in places.

6   Mix the crème fraîche and soft cheese together with a little salt and pepper and spread over the pizza dough but not quite to the edge. Scatter the mushrooms and then the mozzarella over. Make 4 indentations in the topping and break an egg into each. Drizzle with a little olive oil.

7   Cook on CONVECTION 220°C for 15 minutes or until the cheese is melted, the edges are golden and the eggs are just set (cook a little longer for harder eggs). Serve cut into quarters so that each person gets an egg.

VARIATION

Fiorentina pizza

Make and bake the base as main recipe but spread with 4 tbsp tomato purée and sprinkle with 1 tsp dried oregano. Scatter 200g wilted, well-drained spinach over the tomato and make 4 'nests' in it. Sprinkle all over with 50g grated Cheddar cheese and then 100g grated Emmental or mozzarella. Break an egg into each 'nest', season well and bake as before.

MICRO-QUESADILLAS

These make a delicious change from toasted sandwiches for a snack or light lunch. This is my favourite filling, but you can make with only cheese (the key ingredient) or add some chopped, sun-dried tomato. Also try any charcuterie or even mashed avocado.

Serves 4

4 flour tortillas (plain or wholemeal)
4 slices of ham
100g grated Cheddar cheese

1   Place 1 tortilla on the grill rack on the metal tray, if necessary, on the turntable and GRILL on HIGH (1) for 1 minute until just slightly toasted. Remove from the oven and repeat with one more tortilla.

2   Cover the untoasted sides of each with half the ham and top with a layer of half the grated cheese. Press an untoasted tortilla firmly over each.

3   Place one 'sandwich' on the rack, toasted side down, and cook on COMBINATION: GRILL + MEDIUM (50–60 per cent) for 2 minutes until the cheese has melted, pressing down with a fish slice halfway through cooking. Slide onto a plate and press down firmly with a fish slice again.

4   Repeat with the second 'sandwich'. Cut the micro-quesadillas into wedges to serve.

MEAT MAIN MEALS

As I explained earlier (*see* how microwaves work, page 7), meat cooked using only microwaves cooks quickly, but without an external source of heat it will not brown and crisp on the surface. Microwaves on their own also cook so fast that tougher cuts cannot be tenderised, so for stews and casseroles combination cooking is a much better idea. Fatty meats such as bacon rashers, however, will brown and crisp as the fat becomes hot very quickly, but it's easy to overcook them. The combination cooker is much quicker for cooking meat than a conventional oven and the results are always succulent, with skin crisping beautifully. In this section, you'll find a great selection of dishes, some using convection and microwave, others grill and microwave, and one or two where a microwave alone will do the job. All demonstrate just how versatile your combination cooker can be.

LAMB STEAKS WITH HARISSA
AND SOYA BEANS

I love the fire of harissa with the sweetness of lamb. If you don't like your food very spicy, halve the quantity of the harissa paste.

Serves 4

450g waxy new potatoes, cut into bite-sized pieces
2 good-sized turnips, peeled and cut into bite-sized chunks
Salt and freshly ground black pepper
120ml boiling water
4 lamb steaks
1 tbsp olive oil
1 tbsp harissa paste
200ml chicken stock
1 tbsp tomato purée
½ tsp dried oregano
130g frozen soya beans

To garnish
Torn coriander leaves

To serve
A mixed salad

1   Put the potatoes and turnips in a microwave-safe shallow dish and add a pinch of salt and the boiling water. Cover with a lid or plate and MICROWAVE on HIGH (100 per cent) for 10–12 minutes until tender. Remove from the oven and set aside in their water.

2 Put the lamb steaks in a shallow ceramic dish that's big enough to hold them in a single layer. Brush all over with the oil and spread with 2 tsp of the harissa paste on both sides. Place on the rack on the metal tray on the turntable and cook on GRILL (1) for 6 minutes each side until browned and tender but still pink inside.

3 Remove from the oven, lift out the steaks and wrap in foil to rest. Strain the potato water into the dish. Blend in the chicken stock, remaining harissa paste, tomato purée and oregano and add the soya beans. Place on the turntable and MICROWAVE on HIGH for 10 minutes. Remove from the oven.

4 Pop the covered dish of potatoes and turnips on the turntable and MICROWAVE on HIGH for 2 minutes to heat through. Pour any juices from lamb into the soya bean sauce, then put the lamb in warm shallow dishes or on plates and spoon over the sauce. Scatter the potatoes and turnips around, garnish with torn coriander leaves and serve with mixed salad.

SAUSAGES WITH LEEK MASH

If you like a more moist dish, make some Gravy-to-go (*see* page 188) before you prepare the dish, and reheat it on MICROWAVE on HIGH for 1–2 minutes while dishing up the rest of the meal.

Serves 4

600g potatoes, peeled and cut into walnut-sized pieces
2 large leeks, trimmed and chopped
Salt and freshly ground black pepper
150ml boiling water
8–10 thick, good-quality pork sausages (depending on appetites)
Large knob of butter
2 tbsp milk
1 tbsp grainy mustard
300g frozen peas

1   Put the potatoes and leeks in a large microwave-safe dish with a pinch of salt and the boiling water. Cover with a lid or cling film rolled back slightly at one edge. Place on the turntable and MICROWAVE on HIGH (100 per cent) for 15 minutes, stirring once or twice until the vegetables are tender.

2   Drain off the water then re-cover, top with foil or a tea towel to insulate and leave to stand while cooking the sausages.

3   Place the sausages on the high rack over the metal tray on the turntable. Prick with a fork in several places. GRILL on HIGH (1) for 16–18 minutes, turning over halfway through cooking, then wrap in foil and set aside.

4   Mash the potatoes and leeks with the butter and milk then beat in the grainy mustard. Taste and re-season if necessary. Put the peas in a microwae-safe shallow dish with 3 tbsp boiling water. MICROWAVE on HIGH for 3–4 minutes, stirring once. Remove and leave to stand while you MICROWAVE on HIGH the mashed potato in the covered dish for 1 minute to reheat.

5   Spoon the mash onto warm plates. Top with the sausages and place the peas on one side.

BEEF, SPINACH AND MOZZARELLA LASAGNE

This lasagne has a delicious added layer of spinach and mozzarella. As lasagne takes a bit of preparation, I like to make enough for two dishes then freeze one, unbaked, for another day. If you prefer, halve the quantities to make just one.

Serves 4 (each dish)

600ml (2 quantities) cheese sauce (*see* page 187)
250g leaf spinach
2 large tomatoes, chopped
Freshly grated nutmeg
Salt and freshly ground black pepper
2 tbsp olive oil
2 onions, finely chopped
2 garlic cloves, crushed
1 large carrot, chopped
500g lean minced beef
120g mushrooms, sliced
400g can chopped tomatoes
150ml beef stock
2 tbsp tomato purée
A good pinch of caster sugar
1 bay leaf
1 tsp dried oregano
16–20 green lasagne sheets
150g mozzarella, grated
1–2 tbsp grated Parmesan cheese

1   Make the cheese sauce, cover with a circle of wet greaseproof paper and set aside.

2 Put the spinach in a large microwave-safe bowl. Place on the turntable and MICROWAVE on HIGH (100 per cent) for 3 minutes until wilted. Drain, squeeze out all excess moisture with the back of a spoon then snip with scissors. Stir in the chopped fresh tomatoes, a good grating of nutmeg and a little salt and pepper. Set aside.

3 Mix the oil with the onion, garlic and carrot in a large bowl, place on the turntable and MICROWAVE on HIGH for 2 minutes, to soften.

4 Add the beef and MICROWAVE on HIGH for 3 minutes, stirring and breaking up the meat each minute, until browned and all the grains are separate.

5 Add the mushrooms, chopped tomatoes, stock, tomato purée, sugar, herbs and a little salt and pepper and MICROWAVE on HIGH for 10 minutes until rich and thick, stirring once.

6 Spoon a little of the meat sauce in the base of two rectangular 1.5–2-litre ovenproof dishes.

7 Add a layer of lasagne sheets, then add half the beef mixture, divided between the two dishes. Top with another layer of lasagne, all the spinach mixture divided between the two, then all the mozzarella, again divided between the two dishes. Repeat with a layer of lasagne then a layer of meat, finishing with a layer of lasagne. Spoon the sauce over and top with a little grated Parmesan.

8 Place on the metal tray or low rack on the turntable and bake on COMBINATION: CONVECTION 180°C + MEDIUM (50–60 per cent) for 20 minutes until tender and golden on top. If over-browning, cover with a smooth sheet of foil, pressing down round the rim so that it doesn't touch the sides of the oven for the last 5 minutes.

BEEF AND PEPPER BURRITOS

Try adding a dollop of guacamole (or simply some avocado mashed with a dash of lemon or lime juice) to each burrito with the soured cream and cheese. The beef mixture is also good served spooned over rice.

Serves 4

2 tbsp olive oil
250g steak stir-fry strips
1 garlic clove, crushed
3 tbsp water
2 tbsp tomato purée
1 tbsp Cajun spices
Salt and freshly ground black pepper
1 red pepper, halved, seeded and sliced
1 green pepper, halved, seeded and sliced
1 yellow pepper, halved, seeded and sliced
1 bunch of spring onions, trimmed and chopped
2 courgettes, sliced
2 tbsp chopped fresh coriander (optional)
8 corn and wheat tortillas

To serve
Soured cream or crème fraîche
100g Cheddar cheese, grated

1 Put 1 tbsp of the oil and the steak strips in a large microwave-safe bowl and toss to coat. MICROWAVE ON HIGH (100 per cent) for 3 minutes, stirring once.

2 Stir in the garlic, water, tomato purée and spices, season with salt and pepper, then mix in the vegetables and drizzle with the remaining oil. Stir well. Cover with a plate or cling film rolled back slightly at one edge and MICROWAVE on HIGH for 5 minutes. Stir well then MICROWAVE uncovered on HIGH for a further 10 minutes, or until the vegetables are tender but still with a little bite and bathed in sauce, stirring once halfway through cooking. Taste and re-season if necessary. Remove from the microwave, stir in the coriander and cover with foil.

3 Wrap the stack of tortillas in kitchen paper and place on the turntable. MICROWAVE on HIGH for 1 minute, turning the stack over after 30 seconds, to warm. Divide the mixture between the tortillas. Top with a spoonful of soured cream or crème fraîche, and some grated cheese. Fold the wraps over the filling and serve.

VARIATION

Enchiladas

Prepare as above but divide the mixture among the tortillas, roll up and pack into a shallow ovenproof dish. Make 300ml Cheese sauce (*see* page 187), spoon over the tortillas and sprinkle with the grated cheese. Place on the metal tray or low rack on the turntable and cook on COMBINATION: CONVECTION 190°C + MEDIUM-LOW/SIMMER (25–30 per cent) for 10 minutes until turning golden on top.

STUFFED AUBERGINES

This is a great way to use up leftover beef or lamb from a Sunday roast. If you don't have any, you can use 225g fresh minced meat and simply fry it off with the onions first until cooked, then stir well until all the grains are separated before adding the remaining ingredients.

Serves 4

2 aubergines, trimmed and halved lengthways
2 tbsp olive oil
1 onion, chopped
1 garlic clove, crushed
400g can chopped tomatoes
1 tsp ground cinnamon
½ tsp ground cumin
½ tsp dried oregano
A good pinch of caster sugar
Salt and freshly ground black pepper
225g lean roast beef or lamb, cut into small dice or minced
3 tbsp porridge oats
75g feta cheese, crumbled

To serve
Warm wholemeal pitta breads or Quick seed flatbreads
   (*see* page 172)
A crisp mixed salad

1   Prepare the flesh of the aubergines so it will be easy to remove after cooking. With the cut sides up, cut into the aubergine flesh about 5mm in from the edge all the way round, taking care not to cut right through the purple skin underneath. Score the flesh deeply inside the cut line in a criss-cross pattern. Place cut sides down in a shallow dish and add 90ml water. MICROWAVE on HIGH (100 per cent) for about 8 minutes or until soft. Leave to stand for a few minutes until cool enough to handle, drain well then scoop out the soft flesh, leaving the border intact, to form 4 shells. Set the flesh aside and arrange the 4 shells in the shallow dish, add 6 tbsp more water to the dish and set aside.

2   Mix the oil with the onion and garlic and MICROWAVE on HIGH for 2 minutes, stirring once.

3   Add all the remaining ingredients, including the diced aubergine flesh but not the cheese, and MICROWAVE on HIGH for 10 minutes, stirring twice until thick and pulpy. Taste and re-season the filling if necessary.

4   Spoon the filling into the aubergine shells, and pack in well. Scatter the feta cheese over the top. Place on the metal rack or a baking sheet that will fit on the low rack, place on the turntable and cook on COMBINATION: CONVECTION 190°C + LOW/WARM (10 per cent) for 15 minutes until bubbling and turning just slightly golden on top.

5   Leave to cool for 10 minutes (the flavour is better if not searing hot!) while you heat the pitta or flatbreads briefly in the microwave. Serve the aubergines with the warmed bread, cut into strips, and a mixed salad.

KEEMA CURRY WITH RAITA

I like peas and courgette in this but you could add broad beans, diced carrot or even some other roots, like swede or parsnip. If you prefer, you can serve the curry on a bed of plain basmati rice rather than with naan bread.

Serves 4

For the curry
1 tbsp sunflower oil
1 onion, chopped
2 garlic cloves, crushed
500g lean minced lamb
2 tbsp Madras curry paste
2 tsp grated fresh root ginger
150ml chicken or lamb stock
2 tsp tomato purée
150g frozen peas
1 large or 2 small courgettes, diced

For the raita
¼ cucumber, finely diced
2 tsp dried mint
150ml thick plain yoghurt

To serve
4 naan breads (or use the Flatbread recipe on page 172)
2 tbsp chopped fresh coriander
A few salad leaves, tomato wedges, slices of cucumber and
   onion rings

1   Put the oil in a large microwave-safe bowl. Add the onion and garlic and MICROWAVE on HIGH (100 per cent) for 2 minutes to soften.

2   Add the minced lamb and break up well. MICROWAVE on HIGH for 5–6 minutes, stirring twice and breaking up with a spoon until browned and all the grains are separate.

3   Stir in the curry paste and MICROWAVE on HIGH for a further 30 seconds. Add the remaining curry ingredients, stir well and MICROWAVE on MEDIUM (50–60 per cent) for 20 minutes until rich and tender, stirring once. Season to taste with salt.

4   Meanwhile, squeeze out excess moisture from the diced cucumber and place in a small bowl. Stir in the mint and yoghurt and season to taste.

5   When the curry is cooked, cover with foil and leave to stand while you warm the naans. Put the naan breads on the grill rack over the metal tray, if necessary, on the turntable and GRILL on HIGH (1) for 1–2 minutes each side to warm. Spoon the curry into bowls and sprinkle with the coriander. Serve with the raita, salad and warm naan breads.

SLOW-ROAST BELLY PORK
WITH SAGE AND ONION POTATOES

Belly of pork is still an economical cut. Choose a lean piece and make sure you score the rind deeply. The huge plus is that I find this cut crisps and crackles beautifully in the combination cooker – something that doesn't always work so well when cooked conventionally.

Serves 4

600g piece boned belly pork
Salt and freshly ground black pepper
1 onion, chopped
1 large carrot, cut in small dice
½ small celeriac, cut in small dice
150ml dry white wine
300ml pork or chicken stock
1 bay leaf
500g new potatoes, washed and cut into bite-sized chunks
2 red onions, each cut into 6 wedges
2 tbsp olive oil
1 tbsp chopped fresh sage, or 1 tsp dried

To serve
A crisp green salad

1   Wipe the pork well with kitchen paper to dry it and score the rind deeply in a criss-cross pattern. Rub a little salt into the skin and place in a microwave-safe roasting dish.

2   Spread the chopped onion, diced carrot and celeriac around the meat. Pour the wine and stock over the vegetables. Add the bay leaf.

3   Cook on the metal tray or low rack on the turntable on COMBINATION: CONVECTION 150°C + LOW/WARM (10 per cent) for 1 hour until the pork and vegetables are tender and the crackling has crackled. Cover with foil and set aside.

4   Spread the potatoes out in a shallow baking tin. Add the red onions, drizzle with olive oil and toss well. Sprinkle with the sage and some salt and pepper. Place on the metal tray or low rack on the turntable and cook on COMBINATION 220°C + MEDIUM (50–60 per cent) for 20 minutes until tender, stirring and turning once or twice during cooking.

5   Remove the meat from the dish. Pop the juices and vegetables back in the oven in the turntable and MICROWAVE on HIGH (100 per cent) for 1 minute.

6   Meanwhile, cut the pork into thick slices. Remove the braised vegetables from the juices with a slotted spoon and place on warm plates. Top with the pork. Serve with the sage and onion potatoes and the cooking juices spooned over, with a crisp green salad.

TAGLIATELLE WITH MEATBALLS

The meatballs can be made in advance, then simply heated in the sauce when you are ready to serve. They also make great snacks, served on cocktail sticks with a dip of, perhaps, some tomato ketchup or even guacamole.

Serves 4

1 quantity fresh tomato sauce (*see* page 190)

For the meatballs
1 large shallot or small onion, grated
1 garlic clove, crushed
500g lean minced veal or pork
½ tsp dried chilli flakes (optional)
1 tbsp fresh chopped or 1 tsp dried sage
1 tbsp grated Parmesan cheese, plus extra to serve
Salt and freshly ground black pepper
1 egg, beaten

To finish:
2 tbsp olive oil
400g dried tagliatelle
Boiling water

1   Prepare the tomato sauce and set aside.
2   Mix the grated shallot, crushed garlic, meat, chilli, if using, the sage, 1 tablespoon of grated Parmesan and some salt and pepper thoroughly together then add the beaten egg to bind. Shape into 24 small balls.

3   Brush a large shallow ovenproof and microwave-safe dish with oil and arrange the balls in it. Brush with the remaining oil. Place on the metal tray or the low rack on the turntable and cook on COMBINATION: CONVECTION 190°C + LOW/WARM (10 per cent) for 10 minutes, until cooked through and lightly browned. Drain off the excess liquid and oil and pop the meatballs into the tomato sauce. Set aside.

4   Put the tagliatelle in a large bowl and cover generously with boiling water (you'll need about 1.5 litres). Add a pinch of salt. MICROWAVE on HIGH (100 per cent) for 8 minutes, stirring once or twice, until just tender. Leave to stand while you reheat the meatballs.

5   To reheat the meatballs in the tomato sauce, place on the turntable and MICROWAVE on HIGH for 3 minutes until piping hot all the way through.

6   Drain the tagliatelle then pile onto warm plates. Top with the meatballs in the tomato sauce and serve sprinkled with Parmesan cheese.

PORK STEAKS WITH SWEET AND SOUR VEGETABLES AND 'FRIED' RICE

This makes a delicious change from plain cooked pork or bacon steaks and is a great way of getting more of those five-a-day into the family. Ring the changes with thin strips of carrot or courgette instead of the mangetout, if you prefer.

Serves 4

For the sauce
1 bunch of spring onions, trimmed and cut into short lengths
100g mangetout, trimmed
1 red pepper, seeded and diced
¼ cucumber, cut into 5mm wide batons
225g can pineapple pieces in natural juice
1 tbsp tomato purée
1 tbsp red wine vinegar
1 tbsp soy sauce, plus extra for seasoning
2 tsp clear honey
2 tbsp cornflour

For the rice
1 tbsp sunflower or sesame oil
225g cooked long-grain rice
1 tsp Chinese five-spice powder
5 tbsp cooked (or thawed frozen) peas
1 egg, beaten

To finish:
4 thin loin pork or bacon steaks

1   Start by making the sauce. Put the raw vegetables in a large microwave-safe casserole with 4 tbsp water. Cover and MICROWAVE on HIGH (100 per cent) for 6 minutes, stirring once or twice until just tender but still with some 'bite'.

2   Drain off half the pineapple juice into a small bowl. Add the pineapple and remaining juice to the cooked vegetables with the tomato purée, vinegar, soy sauce and honey.

3   Blend the cornflour with the reserved pineapple juice and stir into the bowl of cooked vegetables. MICROWAVE on HIGH for 3 minutes, stirring once until thickened and clear. Cover with the lid and some foil for extra insulation and set aside.

4   Mix the oil, rice, spice powder and peas together in a shallow dish. Cook on COMBINATION: CONVECTION AT 190°C + LOW/WARM (10 per cent) for 5 minutes. Stir well then push the rice mixture to one side of the dish and pour the egg into the space. Cook on COMBINATION: CONVECTION 190°C + MEDIUM (50–60 per cent) for a further 2 minutes or until the egg is set. Break up the egg and stir it through the rice. Season with a little soy sauce to taste and stir again. Cover with foil and set aside to keep warm.

5   Place the pork steaks on the high rack over the metal tray, or a plate, if necessary, on the turntable. Brush with a little oil then a little soy sauce. GRILL on HIGH (1) for 6 minutes.

6   Place the sauce on the turntable and MICROWAVE on HIGH for a minute or two to reheat. Place the pork on 4 plates, spoon the sauce over and serve the rice to one side.

PORK STIR-FRY WITH GARLIC AND GINGER

This is so quick it makes an ideal meal on a busy weeknight. I've used ready-to-wok noodles for speed but they are relatively expensive, so, if you prefer, simply cook egg noodle nests (*see* page 39). See my notes on the recipes on page 31, too, on using ready-prepared garlic and ginger pastes. If you use an economy pack of veggies, some pieces might be a bit large – broccoli florets, for instance – so take the time to cut them into smaller pieces for even cooking.

Serves 4

2 tbsp sunflower oil
450g pork stir-fry strips
1 tbsp grated fresh root ginger
2 garlic cloves, crushed
450g bag ready-prepared stir-fry vegetables (economy packs are fine)
3 tbsp soy sauce
2 tsp Chinese five-spice powder
90ml water or chicken stock
2 tbsp clear honey
2 x 150g straight-to-wok medium noodles

1   Put the oil in a large microwave-safe dish. Add the meat and toss well to coat. Don't cover. Place on the turntable and MICROWAVE on HIGH (100 per cent) for 3 minutes, stirring once.
2   Add all the remaining ingredients except the noodles and mix well. MICROWAVE on HIGH for 6 minutes, stirring once or twice until tender but the vegetables still have some bite.
3   Crumble in the noodles and MICROWAVE on HIGH for a further 2 minutes. Leave to stand for 2 minutes, then serve in bowls.

CHICKEN AND OTHER POULTRY MAIN MEALS

Chicken is our most popular and versatile bird. Because when skinned it has no visible fat, it doesn't need browning, so works well in the microwave alone. But using the combination cooker means you can have lovely golden-topped bakes and crisp-coated escalopes as well as gloriously browned roasts. Chicken is naturally tender and therefore doesn't require long, slow cooking – the only danger with microwaving is that you can easily overcook it, so timing is of the essence. However, either using the microwave on its own or in combination with convection or grill produces really moist, succulent results when carefully cooked. You'll also find here a couple of great turkey dishes and a main course fusion variation of Peking Duck – a sure favourite with all members of the family.

CHICKEN AND VEGETABLE COUNTRY PIE

This is another dish that includes lots of veggies, so you can just serve it with, perhaps, some crusty bread for a complete meal. I cook the potatoes in a bowl rather than a shallow dish as they are easier to mash that way. Making a well in the centre and arranging them more round the edge of the bowl helps the potatoes to cook more evenly.

Serves 4

750g potatoes, peeled and cut into small chunks
Salt and freshly ground black pepper
55g butter
2 tbsp milk
1 onion, chopped
4 carrots, thinly sliced
½ small white cabbage, finely shredded
100g button mushrooms, left whole or halved, depending on size
85g frozen peas, thawed
1 tsp dried mixed herbs
450ml chicken stock
4 tbsp plain flour
400g diced chicken

1   Put the potatoes in a large microwave-safe bowl with 150ml water and a pinch of salt. Stir and spread them out with a well in the centre. Cover with a plate or cling film rolled back slightly at one edge and MICROWAVE on HIGH (100 per cent) for 10–12 minutes until tender, stirring once. Leave to stand for a few minutes while you start cooking the vegetables, then drain and mash with 25g of the butter and the milk.

2   Put the onion and carrots in a fairly shallow, 2-litre, microwave-safe, ovenproof dish. Add 15g of the butter. Place on the turntable and MICROWAVE on HIGH for 4 minutes, stirring once.

3   Add all the remaining vegetables except the potatoes, some salt and pepper and the herbs. Mix well. Pour over the hot stock and cover with a large plate. Place on the metal tray or low rack on the turntable and cook on COMBINATION: CONVECTION 180°C + MEDIUM-LOW/SIMMER (25–30 per cent) for 15 minutes.

4   Blend the flour with 4 tbsp water and stir into the vegetables, then add the chicken, pushing it down well into the liquid. Re-cover, return to the oven and cook for a further 15 minutes until the vegetables are tender. Stir well, taste and re-season.

5   Spoon the mashed potatoes over the chicken and vegetables to cover completely. Rough up with a fork, then dot all over with the remaining butter. Place on the high rack, on the metal tray if necessary, on the turntable and GRILL on HIGH (1) for 5 minutes until golden.

SUNDAY ROAST CHICKEN

I like to cook some broccoli or another green vegetable conventionally on the hob whilst cooking the rest of the meal in the combination cooker, but you could MICROWAVE your chosen veg on HIGH (100 per cent) for a few minutes until tender first, set it aside, then just reheat briefly while carving the chicken.

Serves 4

500g floury potatoes, peeled, cut into large chunks
200g baby chantenay carrots, topped and tailed
1 large parsnip, peeled, halved widthways and cut into
   thick sticks
Salt and freshly ground black pepper
1.2kg oven-ready chicken
Sprig of thyme or rosemary
3 tbsp olive or sunflower oil
3 tbsp plain flour
Chicken stock, as necessary
A splash of soy sauce

To serve
A green vegetable (*see* intro above)

1   Put the potatoes, carrots and parsnips in a microwave-safe shallow dish with 150ml boiling water and a pinch of salt, cover with a lid or cling film rolled back at one edge and MICROWAVE on HIGH (100 per cent) for the 5 minutes. Alternatively, put them in a pan of lightly salted water on the hob, bring to the boil and boil for 3 minutes. Set aside.

2   Wipe the chicken inside and out with damp kitchen paper, then pull off any fat attached just inside the edge of the body cavity and discard. Push the herbs into the cavity and place breast-side down in a roasting tin. Rub the skin all over with a little of the oil and season with salt.

3   Place on the metal tray or low rack on the turntable and cook on COMBINATION: CONVECTION 190°C + MEDIUM (50–60 per cent) for 15 minutes. Carefully turn the bird over and cook for a further 15 minutes or until brown and the juices run clear when pierced right through the thickest part of the leg with a skewer. Remove from the oven, cover with foil and a tea towel and leave to stand while cooking the roasted vegetables.

4   Drain the par-boiled vegetables, reserving the vegetable water for the gravy, and place in the largest roasting tin that will fit on the turntable. Spread the vegetables out and toss well in the remaining oil. Place on the metal tray or the low rack on the turntable and cook on COMBINATION: CONVECTION 220°C + LOW/WARM (10 per cent) for 30 minutes, turning once, until golden and cooked through. Remove from the oven, cover with foil and set aside to keep warm.

5   Carefully transfer the chicken to a warm carving dish. Spoon off any fat from the juices then pour them into a microwave-safe jug. Blend the flour with a little of the reserved vegetable water until smooth and stir into the jug with the remaining water and stock, if necessary, to make up to 450ml. Add the soy sauce. MICROWAVE on HIGH for 3 minutes, stirring once or twice, until boiling, thickened and smooth.

6   Carve the chicken and serve with the roast vegetables, gravy and a green vegetable.

CHICKEN, BACON AND SWEETCORN CASSEROLE

Although this has a splash of white wine in it, it's a very simple family-friendly recipe that is quick and easy to make. If you choose to serve jacket potatoes with it, cook them first (*see* sardine and cheese jackets, page 126) and wrap them in foil to keep warm while you cook the casserole (they'll stay hot for up to an hour).

Serves 4

350g diced chicken breast
1 shallot, finely chopped
75g diced bacon or pancetta
30ml sunflower oil
100g chestnut mushrooms, quartered
400g can chopped tomatoes
3 tbsp red, white or rosé wine
320g can sweetcorn (including any juice)
Salt and freshly ground black pepper
1 bouquet garni sachet

To serve
Jacket potatoes
A crisp, green salad

1   Put the chicken, shallot and bacon in a microwave-safe, ovenproof casserole and toss in the oil. Place on the turntable and MICROWAVE on HIGH (100 per cent) for 4 minutes, stirring once after 2 minutes.

2   Add all the remaining ingredients and push everything down well in the juice. Place on the metal tray or low rack on the turntable and cook on COMBINATION: CONVECTION 180°C + MEDIUM-LOW/SIMMER (25–30 per cent) for 20 minutes until tender and bubbling.

3   Discard the bouquet garni, taste and re-season if necessary.

CHICKEN, VEGETABLE AND CHORIZO PAELLA

To get a really authentic paella texture, use a round-grain paella rice, such as bomba, but it's fine to use ordinary long-grain if you prefer. Although I say 'authentic', traditional Valencian paella never contains chorizo – and it certainly isn't cooked in a microwave. However, that said, this makes a really tasty Spanish rice dish that I am very happy to call a paella!

Serves 4

1 onion, chopped
2 garlic cloves, crushed
2 carrots, finely diced
1 green pepper, finely diced
3 tbsp olive oil
4 boned chicken thighs, cut into chunks
250g paella rice
½ tsp smoked paprika
½ tsp ground turmeric
1 tsp dried oregano
750ml hot chicken stock
100g cooking chorizo, skinned and cut into thick slices
75g frozen peas
Salt and freshly ground black pepper
1 bay leaf

To serve
Lemon wedges
A mixed salad

1   Put the onion, garlic, carrot, pepper and 2 tbsp of the olive oil in a large shallow microwave-safe, ovenproof dish. Stir well. Place on the turntable and MICROWAVE on HIGH (100 per cent) for 2 minutes.

2   Add the chicken and remaining oil and turn to completely coat the chicken. MICROWAVE on HIGH for 2 minutes. Remove the chicken from the dish.

3   Add the rice, paprika, turmeric, oregano, stock, chorizo and peas. Stir well. Replace the chicken, pushing it well down in the dish. Season well and tuck in the bay leaf. Do not cover.

4   Place in the oven on the metal tray or low rack on the turntable. Cook on COMBINATION: CONVECTION 180°C + LOW/WARM (10 per cent) for 35 minutes until slightly crusty around the edges, the liquid has almost been absorbed and the rice and chicken are tender. Discard the bay leaf. Serve hot with lemon wedges to squeeze over and a mixed salad.

CHICKEN, MUSHROOM AND REDCURRANT PASTIES

This is very 'Seventies' but is still a great way to use up leftover chicken or turkey and make a little meat go a long way. I like to serve with new potatoes and peas. If you like extra sauce, heat the remaining soup with a pinch more dried mixed herbs to serve with the pasties. They are also good cold, so ideal to pack in lunchboxes.

Serves 4

200g cooked leftover chicken, cut into small neat pieces
100g mushrooms, diced
1 shallot, finely chopped
½ tsp dried mixed herbs
½ x 400g can cream of mushroom soup
Freshly ground black pepper
500g shortcrust pastry
4 tsp redcurrant jelly
1 egg, beaten

1　Mix the chicken with the mushrooms, shallot, herbs and soup. Season well with pepper.
2　Preheat the oven to CONVECTION 200°C. Cut the pastry into quarters and roll out each piece to an 18cm square (approximately). Put a quarter of the chicken mixture in the centre of each pastry square.

3 Add a spoonful of redcurrant jelly to each and brush all round the edges with beaten egg. Fold over to form triangular parcels, press edges together well and, using the back of a small knife, 'knock up' the pastry (score the two edges together with small slashes), then flute to form attractive sealed edges. Brush with beaten egg.

4 Transfer the pastries to the metal tray or a non-stick baking sheet that will fit the turntable. Make a small slit in the top of each with the point of a knife to allow steam to escape. Place the metal tray on the turntable, or the baking sheet on the low rack on the turntable. Cook in the preheated oven for about 15 minutes until golden. Carefully turn them over and cook for a further 5 minutes to dry out the bases.

NOTE: If your oven has a base element as well as a top one you may not need to turn them over.

CAJUN CHICKEN

This has been a favourite in our household for years and is very easy to make. I used to make my own spice mixture but buying a tin of ready-prepared is just fine. Sometimes I serve it with an avocado salsa: simply finely dice some avocado, cucumber, tomatoes, pepper and onion and mix with some black olives. Moisten with a dash of olive oil and lime juice, then season with a tiny pinch of salt and a sprinkling of dried chilli flakes.

Serves 4

4 chicken portions
1 tbsp olive oil
2 tbsp Cajun spice blend

To serve
Seeded potato wedges (*see* page 139)
A mixed salad
Soured cream or crème fraîche and tomato ketchup

1   Rub the chicken all over with the olive oil and arrange in a shallow microwave-safe, ovenproof dish. Sprinkle liberally all over with the spice blend. Add 6 tbsp water to the dish.

2   Place on the on the metal tray or low rack on the turntable and cook on COMBINATION: CONVECTION 220°C + MEDIUM-LOW/SIMMER (25–30 per cent) for 25 minutes, turning the chicken over after 10 minutes, then turn back after 20 minutes to finally crisp the skin. Cover the dish with foil to keep warm while cooking the wedges.

3   Put the chicken on warm plates and spoon any juices over. Serve with the potato wedges, a mixed salad, and some soured cream or crème fraîche and ketchup to dip the wedges into.

TURKEY, CRANBERRY AND RED CABBAGE CASSEROLE

People tend just to use red cabbage as a pickle or a side dish but it's great as a basis for this delicious casserole, topped with golden sliced potatoes. The juices may bubble up a bit over some of the potatoes but that just gives them more flavour.

Serves 4

40g butter
450g diced turkey breast
1 onion, chopped
1 garlic clove, crushed
½ small red cabbage, shredded
1 large carrot, diced
1 beetroot, diced
300ml boiling chicken stock
2 heaped tbsp cranberry sauce
1 tsp dried or 1 tbsp chopped fresh thyme
1 tbsp fennel seeds
Salt and freshly ground black pepper
3 potatoes, washed and sliced

1 Put half the butter in a microwave-safe, ovenproof casserole and place on the turntable. MICROWAVE on HIGH (100 per cent) for 30 seconds. Add the turkey and stir well. MICROWAVE on HIGH for 2 minutes, stirring once, to seal. Remove from the casserole and set aside.

2 Add the prepared vegetables to the casserole dish, stir well
   and add 4 tbsp of the stock. Cover and MICROWAVE on HIGH
   for 2 minutes.

3 Stir in the cranberry sauce, thyme, fennel seeds and some salt
   and pepper then add the turkey and stir well. Arrange the
   potato slices overlapping to cover the top completely, then
   pour over the remaining stock and dot with the rest of the
   butter. Cover and cook on COMBINATION: 180°C + MEDIUM-
   LOW/SIMMER (25–30 per cent) for 45 minutes until
   everything is cooked through and the potatoes are browned.

THAI-STYLE RED TURKEY CURRY

This dish takes very little preparation and cooks in a very short time. Cook the rice first so it's left to get nice and sticky while you cook the curry. You could substitute the turkey with chicken if you prefer. This is lovely with half a cucumber cut into chunks, or a handful of halved green beans, cooked in a bowl with 3 tbsp water in the MICROWAVE on HIGH (100 per cent) for 3 minutes. Drain, then stir into the curry before serving.

Serves 4

250g jasmine rice
750ml boiling water
Salt

For the curry
1 bunch spring onions, trimmed and cut into short lengths
1 red pepper, seeded and diced
100g chestnut mushrooms, sliced
1 tbsp sunflower oil
1 tsp grated fresh ginger
1 garlic clove, crushed
2 tbsp Thai red curry paste
400ml can coconut milk
400g diced turkey breast steak
2 tomatoes, quartered
50g raw cashew nuts (or peanuts)
2 tbsp roughly chopped fresh coriander

1   Put the rice in a large bowl with the boiling water and a pinch of salt. Stir, place on the turntable and MICROWAVE on HIGH (100 per cent) for 12 minutes. It should be moist but most of the water absorbed. Remove, stir, cover with foil and leave to stand while cooking the curry (the rice should become soft and sticky).

2   Put the spring onions, red pepper and mushrooms in a microwave-safe, ovenproof casserole and toss in the oil. Place on the turntable and MICROWAVE on HIGH for 5 minutes or until softened.

3   Stir in the ginger, garlic, curry paste and coconut milk, then add the turkey, making sure it is pushed down well into the liquid. Cover with the lid.

4   Place on the metal tray or low rack on the turntable and cook on COMBINATION: CONVECTION 160°C + LOW/WARM (10 per cent) for 25 minutes until the turkey is cooked through and the vegetables are tender. Stir in the tomatoes and nuts and leave to stand for 2 minutes. The mixture should be runny, not thick.

5   Spoon the rice in serving bowls. Top with the curry and all its lovely coconut juices and sprinkle with the coriander.

TURKEY, CHEESE AND HAM ESCALOPES

Prepare the escalopes ready for cooking and chill them while you make the potato dish, then keep the cooked potatoes warm by covering in foil while you cook the escalopes. You can always dish them up and give them a quick blast in the microwave when ready to serve, if you prefer. If you like a sauce with your meal, the Fresh tomato sauce on page 190 works well with these, but omit the tomatoes from the potato accompaniment or serve mashed ones instead.

Serves 4

4 turkey breast steaks
4 slices of Emmental or Leerdammer cheese
2 slices of unsmoked ham
4 tbsp plain flour
Salt and freshly ground black pepper
1 large egg, beaten
80g dried breadcrumbs
Sunflower oil

To serve
Combi-sautéed potatoes with tomatoes and rosemary
  (*see* page 140)
Green beans

1   Put the steaks one at a time in a plastic bag and beat with a meat mallet or rolling pin until flattened and quite thin. Cut each escalope in half widthways and trim off any sinews. Sandwich each pair of halved escalopes with a slice of cheese, folded in half lengthways, and half a slice of ham, cutting to fit but making sure there is an edge of turkey all round the filling so it will seal well. You may find some turkey steaks break up slightly when you flatten them; simply patch together when you make into the sandwiches.

2   Dip each in well-seasoned flour, then beaten egg and then breadcrumbs to coat completely. Arrange on the oiled metal tray, or an oiled baking sheet that will fit on the low rack.

3   Place on the turntable and cook on COMBINATION: CONVECTION 220°C + LOW/WARM (10 per cent) for 10 minutes. Turn over and cook for a further 10 minutes or until crisp on the outside and cooked through. Serve hot with the potatoes and green beans.

GIANT DUCK PANCAKES
WITH FRESH PLUM SAUCE

Peking duck is a family favourite, but it is quite time consuming to make in the traditional way, and the tiny rice pancakes mean that you only get teeny mouthfuls at a time. We love to have ours in flour tortillas instead for a mighty main meal. Serve with a salad of fresh beansprouts and shredded red pepper, dressed with a splash of white balsamic and soy sauce. You can always cook the duck in advance, then when pulled off the bones simply reheat it briefly in the microwave in a covered microwave-safe dish and warm the sauce in a separate dish.

Serves 4

4 duck leg portions
120ml boiling chicken stock
2 garlic cloves, crushed
2 tbsp soy sauce
1 tsp Chinese five-spice powder
4 ripe plums, chopped
2 tsp grated fresh root ginger
4 tbsp plum jam
8 flour tortillas
1 bunch spring onions, trimmed and shredded
1 cucumber, cut into quarters widthways and then in thin strips

1   Put the duck pieces in a microwave-safe, ovenproof dish that will hold them in a single layer. Mix the stock, half the garlic, the soy sauce and five-spice powder together and spoon over. Cover with a lid or plate and place on the metal tray or low rack on the turntable. Cook on COMBINATION: 150°C + LOW/WARM (10 per cent) for 1½ hours until really tender and the skin is crispy.

2   Remove from the oven. Lift out the duck, wrap in foil and set aside to keep warm. Spoon off the fat from the juices in the dish. Add the chopped plums and ginger. Place on the turntable and MICROWAVE on HIGH (100 per cent) for 5–7 minutes or until the plums are pulpy (the time will depend on the type of plum and how ripe they are). Stir in the remaining garlic and the jam and MICROWAVE on HIGH for a further 10 minutes or until thick and concentrated.

3   Wrap the tortillas in kitchen paper, place on the turntable and MICROWAVE on HIGH for 30 seconds to warm.

4   Remove all the duck from the bones. Discard the skin, if preferred (it's healthier without but the skin does taste good!), and shred the meat. Spread a little sauce on each tortilla, top with some duck, spring onion and cucumber strips then roll up and devour.

FISH

We should all be eating more fish as it has so many health benefits. It is always quick to cook, but remains succulent and moist if cooked briefly in the microwave or on combination. When microwaving, the secret is to stop when it is just opaque, as it will finish cooking while standing. The wonderful thing about cooking it using the combination method is that you can now have crispy skin on your fillets or golden baked tops to your gratins and pies. When choosing your fish, do make sure it has been fished sustainably: if you buy from the fish counter, this information should clearly be displayed along with the price, and it should also be clear on the labels of prepackaged fresh or frozen fish – look for the Marine Stewardship logo: a white tick on a blue background.

SALMON AND SPINACH STRUDEL

This recipe uses canned pink salmon, which is surprisingly inexpensive and because you eat the bones too, is rich in calcium as well as omega-3 fatty acids – excellent for health and wellbeing. These are good served with a potato salad.

Serves 4

400g fresh spinach, well-washed and drained
2 x 213g (or 1 large 418g) cans pink salmon, drained
4 large rectangular sheets of filo pastry (or 8 smaller
   squares)
50g butter, melted
2 ripe tomatoes, chopped
1½ tsp dried dill
Salt and freshly ground black pepper
250ml passata
4 tbsp crème fraîche

1   Put the spinach in a microwave-safe bowl and MICROWAVE on HIGH (100 per cent) for 2–3 minutes until wilted, stirring once. Drain in a colander then press out all excess moisture with the back of a spoon and chop the spinach with scissors.
2   Preheat the oven on CONVECTION 190°C. Discard the skin from the fish, flake the flesh, including the bones, then set aside.

3   Lay a sheet of filo on a board and brush with melted butter, fold in half widthways to form a square if a large rectangle, or lay another square on top if smaller sheets. Brush with more butter. Scatter on a quarter of the spinach, then top with a quarter of the fish, leaving a wide border all round. Top with a quarter of the chopped tomatoes and ¼ tsp dill, then season well with pepper and just a few grains of salt, if required.

4   Carefully fold in the sides then roll up the strudel and place on the greased metal tray, or a greased baking sheet that will fit the turntable. Make three more strudels the same way.

5   Place the metal tray on the turntable, or the baking sheet on the low rack on the turntable, and cook in the preheated oven for 20 minutes or until golden and crisp. Remove from the oven.

6   Tip the passata into a measuring jug, stir in the crème fraîche, then add the remaining ½ tsp dill. MICROWAVE on HIGH for 2 minutes, stirring once until piping hot. Serve the strudels hot with the passata.

PLAICE STUFFED WITH SARDINES THYME AND LEMON

These are good served with some buttered pasta ribbons or new potatoes (cook them first in the microwave, (*see* Tagliatelle with meatballs, page 90, or Chicken and vegetable country pie, page 96). Alternatively, cook them on the hob while you bake the plaice and prepare a tomato salad. If you select white-skinned fillets, there is no need to skin them as the skin is very soft when cooked.

Serves 4

85g thyme and leek stuffing mix
225ml boiling water
120g can sardines in olive oil
Finely grated zest and juice of 1 lemon
Salt and freshly ground black pepper
3 tbsp chopped fresh parsley
6 small plaice fillets (about 500g), skinned, if the skin is
 black, and halved lengthways
50g butter
1 tbsp pickled capers, chopped

To serve
Buttered pasta ribbons or new potatoes
A tomato salad

1   Make up the stuffing mix with the boiling water and leave to
    stand for 5 minutes.

2   Mash the sardines with their oil and work into the stuffing
    with the lemon zest and a little seasoning. Add 2 tbsp of the
    parsley.

3   Lay the halved plaice fillets on a board, skinned sides up.
    Spread the stuffing over and roll up. Pack into a shallow
    ovenproof dish.

4   Put the butter in a small bowl, place on the turntable and
    MICROWAVE on HIGH (100 per cent) for 50 seconds to melt.
    Stir in the lemon juice, capers and some black pepper and
    spoon over the fish. Cover with a lid or plate.

5   Place on the metal tray or low rack on the turntable, cover
    with a lid or plate and cook on COMBINATION: CONVECTION
    180°C + MEDIUM-LOW/SIMMER (25–30 per cent) for 10
    minutes. Open the door after 8 minutes and remove the lid
    or plate. Serve hot with any juices spooned over and
    sprinkled with the remaining parsley.

SALMON AND AVOCADO PENNE

This is a variation of a dish I created a few years ago when working with the Food Doctor, Ian Marber, but I hadn't made it in a microwave before. It makes a great TV supper as it's piled into bowls and eaten with a fork. It takes just 20 minutes from start to finish! Any leftovers taste good cold, too.

Serves 4

250g wholemeal or high fibre white penne pasta
Salt and freshly ground black pepper
300g salmon fillet, skinned and cut into chunks
150ml chicken stock
1 heaped tsp harissa paste
1 garlic clove, crushed
100g mushrooms, sliced
4 sundried tomatoes in oil, drained and roughly chopped
2 small or 1 large head of pak choi, chopped
1 tbsp chopped pickled gherkins
3 tbsp toasted pine nuts
12 cherry tomatoes, halved
1 avocado, peeled, stoned and diced

To garnish
Fresh basil

1   Put the pasta in a very large microwave-safe bowl. Cover well with boiling water and add a pinch of salt. MICROWAVE on HIGH (100 per cent) for 10–12 minutes (depending on the pasta used), stirring once or twice. Leave to stand for 2 minutes, drain and set aside.

2   In the same bowl, add all the remaining ingredients except the cherry tomatoes and avocado. Cover with a plate or cling film rolled back slightly at one edge and MICROWAVE on HIGH for 5 minutes, gently stirring once until the fish is cooked and the pak choi wilted but still crunchy.

3   Gently fold in the cooked pasta, tomatoes and avocado. Add a pinch of salt and a good grinding of pepper. Return to the oven and MICROWAVE on HIGH for a further 2 minutes. Pile into bowls and garnish with some torn fresh basil. Serve straight away.

COD AND PUY LENTIL BRAISE

Little green puy lentils don't need pre-soaking and so are great for quick lunches and suppers. You can make a delicious meaty alternative by substituting the fish with 225g diced cooking chorizo, bacon or ham. You can, of course, use any white fish instead of cod.

Serves 4

200g puy lentils
1 bunch spring onions, trimmed and chopped
1 garlic clove crushed
2 carrots, diced small
2 celery sticks, chopped
100g fresh or frozen broad beans or peas
900ml hot vegetable stock
75ml cider or apple juice
½ tsp dried oregano
1 tsp clear honey
Salt and freshly ground black pepper
400g cod fillet, cut into bite-sized pieces
2 tbsp chopped fresh parsley

To serve
Crusty bread
A green salad

1   Put everything except the fish and parsley in a microwave-safe casserole dish. Cover and MICROWAVE ON HIGH (100 per cent) for 45 minutes, stirring once until the lentils are just tender but still with some bite and the vegetables are cooked.

2   Gently stir in the fish. Re-cover and MICROWAVE ON HIGH for 2 minutes until the fish is just cooked through. Leave to stand for 5 minutes, then taste and re-season if necessary. Spoon into bowls, sprinkle over the parsley and serve with crusty bread and a green salad.

SARDINE AND CHEESE JACKETS

This makes a simple supper dish that turns the humble sardine into a delicious treat. You can use pilchards if you prefer.

Serves 4

4 baking potatoes, washed
Good knob of butter
2 x 200g cans sardines in tomato sauce
1 green pepper, seeded and chopped
1 spring onion, finely chopped
Salt and freshly ground black pepper
A good pinch of dried chilli flakes (optional)
75g grated Cheddar cheese

To serve
A mixed salad

1   Prick the potatoes all over with a fork. Place on the metal tray or a microwave-safe, ovenproof plate on the turntable. Cook on COMBINATION: CONVECTION 220°C + MEDIUM-LOW/SIMMER (25–30 per cent) for 25 minutes until soft.

2 Remove from the oven and when cool enough to handle, slice in half and scoop out most of the potato into a large bowl, leaving a 5mm lining of potato in the skins.

3 Mash the scooped-out potato well with the butter, then mash in the sardines and their sauce. Add the green pepper and spring onion and season to taste, adding the chilli, if using.

4 Pile back in the skins and place on the metal tray or a baking tray that will fit on the rack. Top each half with some grated cheese. Place the tray on the rack on the turntable and GRILL on HIGH (1) for 5 minutes or until golden and bubbling. Serve hot with a mixed salad.

POLLACK AND PRAWNS
WITH TOMATO AND GARLIC

I love this served spooned over plain rice, but you could also cook pasta shapes and fold them through the mixture just before serving. Pollack is a good choice because it is locally caught and plentiful but you can, of course, substitute any sustainably-caught white fish or use all prawns – or even drained canned tuna for a flavoursome change.

Serves 4

1 tbsp olive oil
1 onion, chopped
2 garlic cloves, crushed
150ml dry white wine
400g can chopped tomatoes
1 tbsp tomato purée
Good pinch of caster sugar
Salt and freshly ground black pepper
½ tsp dried mixed herbs
250g long-grain rice
600ml boiling water
350g pollack fillet, skinned and cut into bite-sized chunks
100g cooked, peeled prawns

To serve
Chopped fresh parsley
A large green salad

1   Put the oil, onion and garlic in a microwave-safe dish, stir well then place on the turntable and MICROWAVE on HIGH (100 per cent) for 2 minutes.

2   Stir in the wine, tomatoes, tomato purée, sugar, some salt and pepper and the herbs. MICROWAVE on HIGH for 10 minutes until thick and pulpy. Remove from the oven and set aside.

3   Wash the rice, put in a large bowl and stir in the boiling water and a pinch of salt. MICROWAVE on MEDIUM (50–60 per cent) for 10 minutes. Remove from the oven, cover with foil and leave to stand while finishing the fish dish.

4   Add the pollack to the tomato mixture and MICROWAVE on HIGH for 3 minutes. Gently stir in the prawns and microwave a further 2 minutes or until the fish is cooked and the prawns are piping hot all the way through. Taste and re-season if necessary. Fluff up the rice with a fork, spoon on plates and top with the fish mixture. Garnish with chopped fresh parsley and serve with a large green salad.

PICKLED MACKEREL WITH ONIONS AND CUCUMBER

You can use herrings instead but my family prefer mackerel as there are fewer bones to contend with! These can be served warm or cold with potatoes and salad and will keep in the fridge for at least 3 days – in fact the flavour improves with keeping. They're also good sliced cold on rye crispbread with hard-boiled eggs.

Serves 4

4 mackerel fillets, thawed if frozen
Coarse sea salt
1 onion, very thinly sliced
1 tsp dried (or 1 tbsp chopped fresh) dill
1½ tsp demerara sugar
2 tsp pickling spice
1 bay leaf
200ml cider vinegar
¼ cucumber, sliced

1   Gently feel the mackerel fillets all over the flesh with your fingers and pull out any remaining bones (this is called 'pin-boning').

2   Sprinkle the mackerel flesh with a few grains of coarse sea salt then lay half the onion slices over them and sprinkle with half the dill. Roll up, skin sides out, and if necessary secure each with a cocktail stick.

3   Pack into a shallow microwave-safe dish, with the tail end underneath. Scatter with the remaining onion and dill and add the sugar, pickling spice, bay leaf and vinegar. Brush any spices off the actual fish so they float in the vinegar (or they will stick to the skin when cooked).

4   Cover with cling film rolled back slightly at one edge or a microwave-safe lid and place on the turntable. MICROWAVE on HIGH (100 per cent) for 5 minutes until cooked through.

5   Remove from the oven and add the sliced cucumber to the hot cooking liquid. Re-cover and set aside. Serve warm or, when cold, chill until ready to serve. Simply lift the fish out of the vinegar with a slotted spoon and serve with the drained sliced cucumber and onion alongside.

TUNA AND SWEETCORN PASTA BAKE

You can't go wrong with this speedy supper dish. You could even make it quicker by using ready-to-wok pre-cooked noodles instead of the standard pasta. Simply chop them up with scissors and crumble them into the sauce with the tuna.

Serves 4

1 quantity cheese sauce (*see* page 187)
200g pasta shapes, preferably wholemeal
Salt and freshly ground black pepper
185g can tuna, drained
320g can sweetcorn, drained
3–4 tomatoes, sliced
50g Cheddar cheese, grated

1   First make the cheese sauce. Cover with wet greaseproof paper or cling film and set aside.
2   Put the pasta in a large microwave-safe bowl. Cover with plenty of boiling water and add a pinch of salt. Place on the turntable and MICROWAVE on HIGH (100 per cent) for 10–11 minutes (cook for the extra minute if using wholemeal), stirring once until just tender. Leave to stand for 2 minutes then drain and tip back in the bowl.
3   Add the tuna, sweetcorn and cheese sauce and mix thoroughly. Season to taste. Transfer to a 1.5-litre shallow ovenproof dish. Top with the sliced tomatoes then the grated cheese. Place on the metal tray or low rack on the turntable and GRILL on HIGH (1) for 15 minutes until golden and bubbling.

VEGETABLE MAINS AND SIDES

A rainbow of vegetables should play a large part in everyone's daily diet. They don't just have to be plain and cooked as accompaniments, but can make delightful main courses too. This section includes some delicious ways of getting all the family to eat more of their five-a-day, some as centre-stage mains and others to complement meat, fish or poultry dishes. Or for a vegetarian option, serve side dishes with poached or fried eggs, or grilled halloumi for a complete meal. Halloumi is one of my favourite cheeses, try sprinkling the grilled slices with deliciously fragrant za'atar, which you can buy with other herb blends in the supermarket, before serving. You will find other suggestions with each recipe.

MIXED VEGETABLE AND TAHINI ORZOTTO

Pearl barley is a great alternative to rice as it remains 'nutty' when cooked so doesn't become stodgy if you leave it a bit too long. Italians might use orzo, which literally means "large rice", but is actually a type of pasta, so don't get confused! The tahini adds a lovely creamy, toasted nut flavour and the spices add warmth rather than fire. This is a complete meal.

Serves 4

A good knob of butter
250g pearl barley
1 leek, chopped
1 large carrot, diced small
½ small swede, diced small
100g frozen soya beans
30g sesame seeds
2 tbsp tahini paste
750ml boiling vegetable stock
¼ tsp ground ginger
A pinch of ground cloves
½ tsp ground cumin
1 tsp dried oregano
Salt and freshly ground black pepper
12 cherry tomatoes, halved
1 tbsp sesame oil (optional)

1 Put the butter in a large microwave-safe and ovenproof casserole and place on the turntable. MICROWAVE on HIGH (100 per cent) for 50 seconds to melt. Add the pearl barley and toss well until glistening.

2 Add the prepared vegetables, soya beans and sesame seeds. Blend the tahini into the stock and add to the vegetables with the spices and oregano. Season well then stir and turn gently until everything is combined. Leave uncovered and MICROWAVE on HIGH for 7 minutes until boiling then cover, reduce power to MEDIUM (50–60 per cent) and cook for a further 30 minutes until the barley has almost absorbed the liquid and all the vegetables are really tender.

3 Remove from the oven, stir in the tomatoes, re-cover and leave to stand for 5 minutes. Taste and re-season if necessary then serve drizzled with the sesame oil, if using.

VEGETABLE LENTIL AND PANEER CURRY

This is a cheap and highly nutritious dish that can be served with basmati rice or naan breads (*or see* flat bread recipe, page 172), warmed briefly in the microwave before serving. This is ideal as a meal on its own but if serving as an accompaniment to a meat or poultry curry, omit the paneer (an Indian cheese readily available in supermarkets).

Serves 4

2 tbsp sunflower oil
1 onion, chopped
1 garlic clove, crushed
2 tbsp Madras curry paste
1 tbsp tomato purée
115g red lentils
1 large potato, peeled and diced
1 large carrot, halved and sliced
1 green pepper, seeded and diced
½ small butternut squash (about 250g), seeded and diced
80g frozen peas
A large handful of raisins
4 tbsp desiccated coconut
Salt and freshly ground black pepper
600ml boiling vegetable stock
225g paneer, diced
2 tbsp mango chutney, any large pieces chopped
1 tbsp garam masala

To garnish
4 tbsp plain yoghurt
2 tbsp chopped fresh coriander

1 Mix the oil with the onion and garlic in a large microwave-safe casserole and place on the turntable. MICROWAVE on HIGH (100 per cent) for 2 minutes.

2 Stir in all the remaining ingredients except the paneer, mango chutney and garam masala. Cover and cook on COMBINATION: CONVECTION 150°C + MEDIUM (50–60 per cent) for 25 minutes, until the lentils have swollen and absorbed most the liquid and all the vegetables are really tender.

3 Remove from the oven, gently stir in the paneer, chutney and garam masala and leave to stand for 5 minutes. Serve in bowls topped with a spoonful of plain yoghurt and some chopped fresh coriander.

POTATO GRATIN

This is good on its own, hot or cold, just with salad, or it can make a delicious side dish with grilled red meat (particularly pork, bacon or venison) or chicken.

Serves 4

A knob of butter
4 large potatoes, scrubbed
2 garlic cloves, crushed
75g grated Emmental cheese
Salt and freshly ground black pepper
2 eggs
600ml milk

1 Grease a 1.5-litre microwave-safe, ovenproof dish with the butter. Prick the potatoes all over with a fork. Place well apart on kitchen paper on the turntable. Cover with another sheet of kitchen paper. MICROWAVE on HIGH (100 per cent) for 8 minutes until almost soft.

2 Remove from the oven and cut into 3–5mm thick slices. Place a layer in the base of the prepared dish. Dot with a third of the garlic, sprinkle a third of the cheese over and season with a little salt and a good grinding of pepper. Repeat the layers twice more, finishing with a layer of cheese.

3 Beat the eggs and milk together and pour over the layers. It should just reach the top of the potatoes.

4 Place on the metal tray or low rack on the turntable, and cook on COMBINATION: CONVECTION AT 190°C + LOW/WARM (10 per cent) for 20 minutes until set and golden brown on top.

SEEDED POTATO WEDGES

These can be served as a side dish, of course, but also with guacamole (mashed avocado and lime juice, with or without chilli added) and some hummus or taramasalata to dip in for a light lunch or supper. Accompany with some cherry tomatoes, cucumber and carrot sticks to balance the meal.

Serves 4

4 good-sized potatoes, washed
2 tbsp olive oil
2 tsp sesame seeds
2 tsp black onion (nigella) seeds
2 tsp cumin seeds
¼ tsp salt

1 Cut the potatoes in half lengthways then cut each half into 6 wedges.
2 Place in a bowl and add the oil. Toss well to coat. Add all the seeds and the salt and toss well with two spoons or a pair of tongs (or you'll get seeds stuck all over your hands).
3 Spread out on the metal tray or a baking sheet that will fit the turntable. Place on the high rack, on the metal tray if necessary, on the turntable. Cook on COMBINATION: CONVECTION 220°C + MEDIUM (50–60 per cent) for 25 minutes until crisp and golden, turning and rearranging once or twice.

COMBI-SAUTÉED POTATOES WITH TOMATOES AND ROSEMARY

These are delicious with any roast or grilled meats or with the turkey escalopes on page 112. They are also good topped with poached eggs (*see* Eggs Royale page 50) for brunch or supper.

Serves 4

750g potatoes, washed and cut into 1 cm cubes
2 tbsp olive oil
1 garlic clove, crushed
1 tbsp chopped fresh rosemary or 1 tsp dried, very finely crushed
Salt and freshly ground black pepper
3 ripe tomatoes, chopped

1 Toss all the ingredients together and place in a roasting tin that will fit comfortably on the metal tray or low rack. Spread them out evenly and season well.
2 Cook on COMBINATION 220°C + MEDIUM (50–60 per cent) for 15 minutes, turning once until golden in places and cooked through.

MUSHROOM AND SOFT CHEESE RISOTTO

Stirring some soft white cheese through this before serving gives added protein and a luscious creamy sauce. Serve it with a crisp green salad to offset the richness. If you want to serve it as an accompaniment to grilled fish or meat, or topped with fried or poached eggs, omit the cheese.

Serves 4

A good knob of butter
1 bunch spring onions, trimmed and chopped
1 garlic clove, crushed
200g chestnut mushrooms, sliced
250g risotto rice
700ml boiling vegetable stock
1 large bay leaf
Salt and freshly ground black pepper
2 heaped tbsp medium-fat white soft cheese
2 tbsp chopped fresh parsley

1   Put the butter, spring onions, garlic and mushrooms in a large bowl. Place on the turntable and MICROWAVE on HIGH (100 per cent) for 4 minutes until softened.
2   Stir in the rice then 300ml of the stock and add the bay leaf. Season lightly with salt and add plenty of freshly ground black pepper. MICROWAVE on HIGH (100 per cent) for 10 minutes. Stir in a further 300ml of stock and MICROWAVE on HIGH for a further 10 minutes. Check after 5 minutes and add a little more stock if necessary (the result should be creamy with a nutty texture, not too stodgy).
3   Remove from the oven and discard the bay leaf. Stir in the cheese and half the parsley, taste and re-season if necessary. Serve in warm bowls, garnished with the remaining parsley.

MICRO-KIMCHI

Kimchi is a spicy fermented cabbage. This microwave version is sped up to accelerate the process of softening the cabbage. However, it will improve if left overnight to ferment fully and can be kept in the fridge for up to a fortnight. Serve this as a snack or as a side dish with grilled meat or a fish dish, such as simple teriyaki salmon – just brush salmon steaks with bottled teriyaki sauce in a shallow ovenproof dish. Place on the high rack, over the metal tray if necessary, on the turntable and GRILL on HIGH (1) for 5–6 minutes until golden and cooked through.

Serves up to 8

1 Chinese cabbage
1 tbsp salt
1 tbsp sesame seeds
1 fat red chilli, seeded and chopped
1–2 tbsp sambal oelek, according to taste
4 tbsp rice vinegar
1 tbsp lime juice
2 tsp shredded fresh root ginger
1 tbsp toasted sesame oil
3 spring onions, trimmed and chopped

1. Trim the stalk end off the Chinese cabbage. Cut the cabbage in half lengthways then each half into 3 long strips. Cut the strips crossways into 2cm chunks. Place in a colander. Sprinkle with the salt and toss well. Leave to stand on the draining board while you make the marinade.

2. Put all the remaining ingredients except the onions in a bowl. Mix well. Place on the turntable and MICROWAVE on HIGH (100 per cent) for 1 minute 30 seconds until boiling.

3. Rinse the cabbage, drain thoroughly and place in a large sealable plastic box. Pour the marinade over and toss well. Click on the lid, turn the box upside down, give it a good shake, turn upright then place on the turntable and loosen the lid but leave on. MICROWAVE on MEDIUM-LOW (25–30 per cent) for 2 minutes.

4. Seal, give another really good shake and leave to stand for at least 3 hours or overnight, shaking and tipping occasionally. If not eating straight away, store in the fridge for up to 2 weeks.

COURGETTES STUFFED WITH CHICKPEAS AND HALLOUMI

This makes an easy supper dish. You just mash together all the ingredients for the filling, pack it into the scooped-out courgettes and pop them in your combination cooker. Nothing could be simpler. Serve with some crusty bread and a mixed salad. If you have some cooked leftover carrots, then you can use those instead of the canned ones. You can also cook dried chickpeas if you prefer (*see* page 41 for the method).

Serves 4

4 large courgettes
400g can chickpeas, drained
300g can carrots, drained
1 garlic clove, crushed
½ tsp ground coriander
2 tbsp chopped fresh coriander
50g halloumi cheese, cut into small dice
2 tbsp sliced black olives
Salt and freshly ground black pepper
A good squeeze of lemon juice
2 tbsp olive oil
A little grated Parmesan

1   Halve the courgettes lengthways and scoop out the soft, seedy centres using a teaspoon. Chop the flesh and place in a bowl.
2   Add the chickpeas and carrots to the courgette flesh and mash well with a fork or potato masher. Stir in the garlic, ground and fresh coriander, the cheese and the olives. Season to taste with salt, pepper and lemon juice.
3   Arrange the courgette halves on the metal tray or a shallow baking tray that will fit the turntable. Pack the filling into the courgettes and drizzle with the olive oil. Place on the turntable and cook on COMBINATION: CONVECTION 160°C + MEDUM (50–60 per cent) for 25–30 minutes until the courgettes are tender and the tops turning lightly golden. Sprinkle with a little grated Parmesan before serving.

BROCCOLI AND PEANUT NOODLES

This is another simple and nutritious family supper dish. If you like more than just a hint of chilli then add more, or omit altogether if you don't like the tickle of fire. You can use cashew nut butter for a more expensive but delicious alternative, and try using roughly chopped stalks of sprouting broccoli when in season.

Serves 4

4 slabs dried medium egg noodles
200g head broccoli, cut into tiny florets
1 red pepper, seeded and diced small
2 tbsp sunflower oil
2 garlic cloves, crushed
¼–½ tsp dried chilli flakes
4 tbsp crunchy peanut butter
2 tbsp soy sauce
1 tbsp clear honey
1 tbsp lime juice
2 spring onions, trimmed and chopped

To serve
A crisp green salad

1   Put the noodles in a large bowl, cover with boiling water and place on the turntable. MICROWAVE on HIGH (100 per cent) for 4 minutes, stirring once. Drain, return to the bowl, cover with foil and set aside.

2   Put the broccoli and red pepper in a large shallow dish, add
    100ml water cover with a plate or cling film rolled back
    slightly at one edge and MICROWAVE on HIGH for 6 minutes,
    stirring once or twice until tender. Leave to stand for 2
    minutes then lift out the broccoli and pepper with a slotted
    spoon and add to the noodles, retaining the cooking water.

3   Stir the garlic, chilli, peanut butter, soy sauce, honey and
    lime juice into the cooking water. MICROWAVE on HIGH for
    2 minutes, stirring after a minute, until bubbling.

4   Add to the noodles, broccoli and pepper. Toss gently but
    thoroughly. Taste and add a splash more soy sauce or lime
    juice if necessary. Pile in bowls, sprinkle with the chopped
    spring onions and serve with a crisp green salad.

GREEN BEANS IN SPICED TOMATO SAUCE

Restaurateur Yotam Ottolenghi first inspired me to try slow-cooking green beans in this way. It seemed alien to me as I usually cook them very quickly to preserve their vibrant colour. However the result was so delicious I decided to create a version to cook in the combination cooker. They are lovely as a side dish with grilled halloumi, fish or meat, or try topping them with poached eggs.

Serves 4

2 tbsp olive oil

1 red onion, halved and thinly sliced

2 garlic cloves, crushed

1 tsp ground cumin

½ tsp dried chilli flakes

A good pinch of ground cloves

2 tsp sweet paprika

500g runner or helda beans, trimmed and cut into 2.5 cm chunks

400g can chopped tomatoes

1 tbsp tomato purée

400ml boiling vegetable stock

Salt and freshly ground black pepper

1   Put the oil, onion and garlic in 2.5-litre casserole dish and place on the turntable. MICROWAVE on HIGH (100 per cent) for 2 minutes. Stir in the spices and MICROWAVE on HIGH for 30 seconds.

2   Add the beans, tomatoes, tomato purée, stock and some salt and pepper. Cover and cook on COMBINATION: CONVECTION 160°C + MEDIUM (50–60 per cent) for 40 minutes until tender and bathed in a rich sauce. Taste and re-season if necessary.

PARSNIP AND WALNUT ROSTI

These make a delicious accompaniment to cold meats. Alternatively, try them topped with some fried or poached eggs or some grilled bacon or sausages for a tasty lunch or supper.

Serves 4

1 large parsnip (about 300g)
2 potatoes (about 225g)
1 small onion
50g walnuts, finely chopped
Salt and freshly ground black pepper
A good grating of fresh nutmeg
2 eggs, beaten
Olive oil, for greasing

1 Peel and coarsely grate the parsnip, potato and onion into a bowl.
2 Add the walnuts, plenty of salt and pepper and the nutmeg. Toss well then mix with the beaten eggs to bind.
3 Divide the mixture into 4 equal portions. Place on the well-oiled metal tray, or a baking sheet on the low rack, on the turntable. Flatten to about 2.5cm thick and make sure the rosti are just separated (they are quite big!). Drizzle with a little olive oil. Cook on COMBINATION: 220°C + MEDIUM (50–60 per cent) for 20 minutes until crisp round the edges and golden.

DESSERTS

Everyone loves desserts and if they don't take hours to cook then it's a boon! Here I've developed some of our family favourites that make good use of the different elements of your combination cooker so you can get an idea of just how versatile it can be. We still have yoghurt and fruit most days for pudding and have these 'proper' nursery-type desserts at weekends and special occasions. Everyone deserves a treat from time to time!

CHOCOLATE PUDDING WITH BUILT-IN CHOCOLATE SPREAD SAUCE

'Steamed' puddings are perfect made in the microwave – they're light, fluffy and moist. To make quick chocolate custard simply whisk a couple of tablespoons of drinking chocolate powder into a 400g can of vanilla custard.

Serves 4—6

3 heaped tbsp dark chocolate spread
2–3 tbsp boiling water
115g butter, softened
115g caster sugar
85g self-raising flour
30g cocoa powder
1 tsp baking powder
2 eggs

To serve
Chocolate custard
Cream or ice cream

1   Put the chocolate spread in a 1.2-litre pudding basin and gently whisk in the boiling water to a smooth consistency that will run off a spoon.

2 Put all the remaining ingredients in a mixing bowl and beat with an electric beater or a wooden spoon until smooth and fluffy.

3 Spoon over the chocolate spread sauce, gently spreading the mixture right to the side of the basin all round so that none of the chocolate spread is visible.

4 Place on the turntable and MICROWAVE on HIGH (100 per cent) for 2½ minutes until risen and firm with a few 'wet spots' on top. Leave to stand for 5 minutes, then turn out into a serving dish and serve with chocolate custard, and cream or ice cream.

VANILLA RICE PUDDING

I prefer my rice pudding creamy without a tough brown skin so cook it solely in the microwave. If you prefer the more traditional brown top, then when cooked, place on the high rack, on the metal tray if necessary, on the turntable and GRILL on HIGH (1) until golden. If you prefer a stodgier rice pudding, increase the quantity of rice to 75g.

Serves 4

50g short-grain pudding rice
410g can evaporated milk
2 tbsp granulated sugar or to taste
½ tsp natural vanilla extract (or ½ vanilla pod, seeds
  scraped into the milk)
A knob of butter

1 Mix the rice with the milk and 1 canful of water in a microwave-safe, ovenproof dish. If time, leave to stand for several hours or overnight (but not vital).

2 Stir in the sugar and vanilla, then dot with the butter. Place on the turntable, cover with a lid or microwave-safe plate and MICROWAVE on HIGH (100 per cent) for 5 minutes. Stir, reduce the power to MEDIUM-LOW/SIMMER (25–30 per cent) and cook for 1 hour until the rice is really soft, stirring regularly to prevent a skin forming, if wished. Leave to stand for at least 10–15 minutes before serving to allow the rice to become thick and creamy.

BRAMLEY AND DRIED FRUIT SLAB

This is really a 'cut-and-come-again' cake. It is delicious warm for dessert with some cream or custard but any leftovers are great cut into smaller squares to serve with a coffee or cup of tea. Use all sultanas, raisins or currants rather than the fruit cake mix if you prefer.

Serves 8—12

A little sunflower oil, for greasing
190g plain flour, plus extra for dusting
3–4 Bramley cooking apples (depending on size, about 900g)
1 tbsp lemon juice
2 eggs
100g light soft brown sugar
120g caster sugar
100g butter, cut into small pieces
75ml single cream
75ml milk
1 tbsp baking powder
75g dried fruit cake mix

1 Grease a baking dish or tin about 23 x 29 x 6cm and dust with flour. Peel, quarter, core and slice the apples and place in a bowl of cold water with the lemon juice added to prevent browning.

2   Break the eggs into a large bowl and add 75g of the brown sugar and all the caster sugar. Whisk until thick and pale and the mixture leaves a trail when the whisk is lifted out of the mixture (an electric beater makes this a lot easier).

3   Put the butter, cream and milk in a separate microwave-safe bowl. Place on the turntable and MICROWAVE on HIGH (100 per cent) for 2 minutes until boiling and the butter has melted.

4   Stir this boiling liquid into the eggs and sugar. Sift the flour and baking powder over the top, scatter over the dried fruit mix and fold in with a metal spoon. Pour into the prepared tin.

5   Drain the apples and arrange in overlapping rows over the cake mixture, then sprinkle with the remaining brown sugar.

6   Place on the metal tray or low rack on the turntable and cook on COMBINATION: CONVECTION 200°C + MEDIUM-LOW/SIMMER (25–30 per cent) for 15 minutes until risen, golden, firm to the touch and the apples are cooked through. Serve warm or cold cut into squares.

NEW YORK-STYLE CHEESECAKE

Rather than the crème fraîche topping I've used here, you can pile on fresh fruit or stewed fruit with arrowroot-thickened juice (or use a can of pie filling).

Serves 6—8

A little sunflower oil, for greasing
75g butter
150g digestive biscuits, crushed
750g medium-fat soft cheese
120g caster sugar
4 eggs, beaten
1 tsp natural vanilla extract

To decorate
150ml crème fraîche

1   Grease and line a 20cm deep, smooth cake tin with baking paper. Put the butter in a bowl and place on the turntable. MICROWAVE on HIGH (100 per cent) for 50 seconds until melted. Stir in the crushed digestive biscuits and press into the base of the prepared cake tin.

2   Beat the cream cheese with the sugar, eggs and vanilla. Spoon into the prepared tin. Place the tin on the metal tray or low rack on the turntable and cook on COMBINATION: CONVECTION 150°C + MEDIUM–LOW/SIMMER (25–30 per cent) for 15 minutes until just beginning to brown and the filling is wobbly.

3   Remove from the oven and take out the metal tray or rack. Place on the turntable and MICROWAVE on MEDIUM-LOW/SIMMER (25–30 per cent) for 10 minutes until set. Remove from the oven and leave to cool completely, then chill.

4   Carefully remove from the tin and swirl the crème fraîche over the surface before serving.

BLACKBERRY APPLE AND ALMOND CRUMBLE

Using a combination of microwave and convection means you can cook the fruit from raw and still have a crisp but not burnt crumble at the end of cooking – and it's much faster than traditional baking, too!

Serves 4—6

500g Cox's or similar eating apples, peeled, quartered, cored and sliced
170g fresh blackberries
100g caster sugar
1 tsp lemon juice
4 tbsp water
75g spelt flour
75g porridge oats
50g butter
25g ground almonds

To serve
Cream, custard or ice cream

1   Mix the sliced apples with the blackberries in a 1.2-litre microwave-safe, ovenproof dish. Add 3 tbsp of the sugar, the lemon juice and water and mix well. Cover with a lid or cling film rolled back slightly at one edge and place on the turntable. MICROWAVE on HIGH (100 per cent) for 5 minutes. Stir well.

2   Meanwhile, put the spelt flour and oats in a bowl and rub in the butter until the mixture resembles breadcrumbs. Stir in the almonds and all but 1 tbsp of the remaining sugar. Scatter over the fruit and press down very lightly. Dust with the remaining sugar.

3   Place on the metal tray or low rack on the turntable and cook on COMBINATION: CONVECTION 170°C + MEDIUM-LOW/SIMMER (25–30 per cent) for 15 minutes until crisp and browned on top and the fruit is completely tender. Serve with cream, custard or ice cream.

CHOCOLATE MOUSSE

In this recipe, the only reason for using your oven is to melt the chocolate and butter but it is quicker than fiddling about with a pan of water on the hob, so it illustrates how versatile your oven can be. Also it is such a family favourite that I couldn't leave it out! Don't give to children under a year old, as the eggs aren't cooked.

Serves 4

150g plain chocolate, plus extra for grating
30g unsalted butter
4 eggs, separated
2 tbsp caster sugar
½ tsp natural vanilla extract
2 tsp brandy (optional)

To decorate
Whipped cream

1   Break up the chocolate and place in a good-sized microwave-safe bowl (large enough to take the whisked egg whites too). Add the butter. Place on the turntable and MICROWAVE on HIGH (100 per cent) for 1 minute 50 seconds. Stir until completely melted.
2   Meanwhile, whisk the egg whites until stiff and whisk in the sugar.
3   Beat the egg yolks, vanilla and brandy, if using, into the melted chocolate.
4   Fold the egg whites into the chocolate with a metal spoon. Divide between 4–6 serving glasses or spoon into a serving dish and chill until firm. Decorate with a dollop of whipped cream and a little grated chocolate before serving.

CRÈME BRÛLÉE

I know this is not a new recipe but it is so incredibly simple to make in your combination oven, I just had to include it. You can flavour with chocolate or coffee (just dissolve a spoonful of cocoa or coffee granules in a little water and whisk into the cream, adding enough of it to give the flavour you like). Don't chill for more than a couple of hours after caramelising or the top will go runny again and the result will be an upside-down crème caramel!

Serves 4

3 eggs
2 tbsp caster sugar
450ml single cream
1 vanilla pod, seeds scraped
6 tbsp light soft brown sugar

1   Whisk the eggs and caster sugar together then whisk in the cream and vanilla seeds.
2   Pour into 4 ramekin dishes. Place the dishes in a flan dish with enough boiling water to come halfway up the sides of the dishes.
3   Place on the turntable and MICROWAVE on MEDIUM-LOW/SIMMER (25–30 per cent) for 8–9 minutes or until just set. Leave to cool, then chill.
4   Sprinkle the tops liberally with the soft brown sugar and place on the high rack, on the metal tray if necessary, on the turntable. GRILL on HIGH (1) for about 8 minutes until melted and caramelised. Remove from the oven and serve straight away, or cool, then chill for up to 2 hours.

PEAR AND CUSTARD CHOCOLATE OAT FLAN

Pears and chocolate have always been a great combination and the oats in the flan case add extra goodness to a delicious tart. It's still a bit of a cheat because I use a can of custard as the base for the filling – and why not?

Serves 6

75g butter
40g caster sugar
50g spelt flour
40g cocoa powder
75g rolled oats
Pinch of salt
A little sunflower oil, for greasing
2 eggs
400g can custard
410g can pear halves
1 tbsp arrowroot

1   Preheat the oven to CONVECTION 200°C. Cream the butter and sugar together until fluffy, then work in the spelt flour, 25g of the cocoa powder, the oats and salt.

2   Grease a 20cm microwave-safe, ovenproof flan dish. Roll out
    the dough on a lightly floured surface and use to line the
    dish (it is quite crumbly, so patch it up as necessary – don't
    worry, it won't show!). If time, chill for 30 minutes to rest.
    Prick the base all over with a fork and line with greaseproof
    paper and baking beans. Place on the metal tray or low rack
    on the turntable and cook in the preheated oven for 10
    minutes. Remove the paper and beans and bake for a further
    5 minutes.

3   Beat the eggs and remaining cocoa powder into the custard
    and spoon into the flan. Return to the oven and cook on
    COMBINATION: 180°C + LOW/WARM (10 per cent) for 15
    minutes or until just set. Remove from the oven and leave to
    cool, then chill until firm.

4   Drain the pear halves, reserving the juice. Slice the fruit and
    dry on kitchen paper. Blend the arrowroot with the pear
    juice in a small bowl. Place on the turntable and MICROWAVE
    on HIGH (100 per cent) for 1 minute or until thickened and
    clear, stirring once. Arrange the pear slices over the custard
    and spoon the thickened juices over to coat completely. Chill
    again until ready to serve.

CAKES AND BAKES

Microwave ovens have always been renowned for making very light sponges but they cannot brown, so you have to use dark mixtures, such as chocolate, use brown sugar instead of white, or devise ways of coating them: sprinkling thickly with demerara sugar before or straight after baking or smothering in icing to disguise their rather anaemic appearance. But now, using your combination cooker, you can get the best of both worlds – light, moist and golden brown cakes and bakes.

SPELT BAKING POWDER BREAD

A no-prove bread is a great extra in any cook's repertoire as it is really quick to make. It's best eaten fresh but will toast beautifully for the next few days as well. I found turning the bread over towards the end was the best way in my oven to get the bread crisp and cooked through without being too brown on the top. However, you may find that if you have an oven with an element top and bottom you don't need to turn it over, in which case cook for 20 minutes then check. If the base sounds hollow when tapped, it is cooked. If not, cook for a few minutes longer.

Makes 1 loaf

100g plain flour
350g spelt flour
1 tsp salt
1 tsp light brown sugar
4 tsp baking powder
30g butter
325ml milk, plus a little extra for brushing
A little sunflower oil, for greasing
1 tbsp rolled oats

1   Preheat the oven to 200°C. Mix all the dry ingredients except the oats in a bowl. Rub in the butter. Stir in the milk to form a soft but not sticky dough.

2   Knead briefly and gently on a lightly floured surface until smooth, then shape the dough into a large ball. Lightly oil the metal tray, or a baking sheet on the low rack, and place the dough on it.

3   Mark and cut a deep cross into the top with a sharp knife. Brush with a little milk and sprinkle with the rolled oats. Place on the turntable and cook on COMBINATION: 200°C + LOW/WARM (10 per cent) for 15 minutes until risen and golden. Turn the bread over and cook for a further 10 minutes or until golden and the base sounds hollow when tapped. Transfer to a wire rack, cover with a clean tea towel to soften the crust slightly and leave to cool. Best served warm.

WHOLEMEAL KNOTS

These are best cooked on convection only but you can use the microwave to speed up the proving time, which is great. Also, as you are only cooking one tray of rolls, it really does save a lot of oven heat being wasted by using your larger conventional oven.

Makes 8

450g strong wholemeal flour
1 tsp salt
1 tbsp dried milk powder (optional)
1 tsp caster sugar
2 tsp easy-blend dried yeast
1 tbsp olive oil
250ml lukewarm water
Beaten egg or plain yoghurt to glaze
Poppy seeds

1   Mix the flour, salt, milk powder, if using, sugar and yeast in a large microwave-safe bowl. Add the oil then the lukewarm water to form a soft but not sticky dough. Knead gently on a lightly floured surface for at least 5 minutes until smooth and elastic. Alternatively, put the flour, salt, milk powder and sugar in the bowl of a food processor with the dough hook attached. Stir in the yeast then add the water with the machine running to form the dough, and run the machine for 2 minutes to knead.

2   Place the dough in a microwave-safe bowl. Cover with a damp cloth. Place on the turntable and MICROWAVE on MEDIUM (50–60 per cent) for 10 seconds. Leave to stand for 3 minutes. Repeat this rising process 6 times or until the dough is spongy and almost doubled in bulk. Alternatively, leave in a warm room to prove for about 1 hour.

3   Divide the dough into 8 even-sized pieces. Roll out each piece into a sausage shape about 20cm long and tie into a knot. Arrange well apart on the greased metal tray, or a greased baking sheet that will fit on the low rack. Repeat the proving process as step 2, 5 times, or leave in a warm place until the rolls have risen.

4   Preheat the oven to CONVECTION 210°C. Lightly brush the rolls with beaten egg or yoghurt and sprinkle with the poppy seeds.

5   Place the metal tray on the turntable, or the baking sheet on the low rack, and cook in the preheated oven for 12 minutes until browned and the bases sound hollow when tapped. Cool on a wire rack.

QUICK SEED FLATBREADS

These are ideal to serve with curries, such as the Keema on page 86, or Middle-eastern dishes, such as the Stuffed aubergines on page 84. They're also great served with hummus or taramasalata and crudités for a quick lunch or you can even use them as mini pizza bases.

Makes 8

275g self-raising flour
150ml plain yoghurt
2 tbsp milk
1½ tbsp sunflower oil
½ tsp salt
½ tsp caster sugar
1 egg, beaten
2 tsp sesame seeds
2 tsp black onion (nigella) seeds

1   Preheat the oven to CONVECTION 220°C. Mix all the ingredients except the sesame and onion seeds in a bowl. Knead gently on a lightly floured surface. Divide into 8 pieces and roll each into a round about 12cm in diameter. Sprinkle with the seeds and roll gently to press them into the surface. Pull one end of each to make the breads droplet shaped.

2   Arrange 4 breads on the metal tray or a non-stick baking sheet that will fit the low rack. Place on the turntable and cook for 5 minutes until puffy and lightly browned in places.

3   Wrap in a clean cloth to keep soft. Repeat with the remaining four breads. Serve warm.

CHEESE AND CELERY SEED SCONES

These are delicious served any time of day – great for breakfast (try them spread with butter and Marmite, if you love it), as an accompaniment to soup for lunch, as a teatime or after-school treat, or instead of bread with a main meal.

Makes 8

225g self-raising flour
A pinch of salt
½ tsp English mustard powder (optional)
1 tsp baking powder
40g butter, plus extra to serve
75g strong Cheddar cheese
1 tbsp celery seeds, plus a few extra for dusting
120ml plain yoghurt
4 tbsp milk, plus extra for brushing

1   Preheat the oven to CONVECTION 210°C. Mix the flour, salt, mustard powder, if using, and baking powder together. Rub in the butter then stir in the cheese and celery seeds. Mix with the yoghurt and milk to form a soft but not sticky dough.

3   Knead briefly on a lightly floured surface and pat out to about 2cm thick. Cut into 8 rounds using a 5cm fluted cutter. Place on the metal tray, lightly greased, or a baking sheet that fits the low rack on the turntable, brush with the extra milk then sprinkle with a few extra celery seeds.

3   Place on the turntable and bake for 12 minutes until risen, browned and the bases sound hollow when tapped. Transfer to a wire rack. Best served warm with butter.

BLUEBERRY AND PISTACHIO MUFFINS

This mixture would make about 8 large muffins, but you'd need to cook them for a minute or two longer. To save a few minutes you can use combination of convection and microwave for these, the same temperature plus LOW/WARM (10 per cent) and cook for 8 minutes, but I found the result a little dry.

Makes 14

60g butter
90g wholemeal flour
75g plain flour
A good pinch of salt
1½ tsp baking powder
100g light soft brown sugar
Finely grated zest of ½ lime
20g pistachio nuts, roughly chopped
100ml plain yoghurt
¼ tsp natural vanilla extract
1 egg, beaten
100g blueberries
2 tbsp demerara sugar for dusting

1 Put the butter in a small microwave-safe bowl and place on the turntable. MICROWAVE ON HIGH (100 per cent) for 30 seconds.
2 Preheat the oven on CONVECTION 180°C. Mix the flours with the salt, baking powder, sugar and lime zest. Stir in the pistachios.

3   Add the melted butter, yoghurt, vanilla and beaten egg and mix to form a soft dropping consistency. Stir in the blueberries.

4   Arrange 7 double-thickness paper cake cases on the metal tray or low rack on the turntable. Spoon in half the muffin mix (they should be almost full). Sprinkle with demerara sugar.

5   Cook for 12 minutes until risen and golden and the centres spring back when lightly pressed. Cool on a wire rack. Remove the outer cake cases and use as the inner cases for the second batch. Repeat with the remaining mixture to make a further 7 muffins.

CARROT AND PARSNIP CAKE

This is another good way to get extra veggies into the kids! Moist and lightly spiced, it makes a delicious teatime treat. Make sure you finely grate the carrot and parsnip, as if it is coarsely grated it won't soften completely in the short cooking time.

Makes 1 x 20cm cake

150ml sunflower oil, plus extra for greasing
3 eggs
225g caster sugar
1 tsp natural vanilla extract
175g self-raising flour
½ tsp bicarbonate of soda
1 tsp ground cinnamon
1 large carrot (about 150g), peeled and finely grated
1 smallish parsnip (about 115g), peeled and finely grated
50g walnuts, chopped, plus a few walnut halves to decorate

For the soft cheese frosting
60g white soft cheese
140g icing sugar, sifted
¼ tsp natural vanilla extract
Finely grated zest of ½ lemon (optional)

1   Grease a 20cm cake tin or soufflé dish and line with baking paper (or use a silicone pan, in which case you need not grease or line). Beat the oil, eggs, sugar and vanilla together.

2 Sift the flour, bicarbonate of soda and cinnamon over, then fold in with a metal spoon. Fold in the carrot, parsnip and walnuts.

3 Turn into the prepared dish and smooth the surface. Place on the metal tray, or a baking sheet that will fit the turntable on the low rack, on the turntable. Cook on COMBINATION: CONVECTION 180°C + MEDIUM-LOW/SIMMER (25–30 per cent) for 14 minutes until richly browned.

4 Remove the metal tray or rack and MICROWAVE on the turntable on MEDIUM (50–60 per cent) for 3 minutes to ensure the centre is cooked through but the cake does not become over-brown. Leave to cool for 10 minutes then turn out onto a wire rack, remove the baking paper and leave to cool completely.

5 To make the frosting, beat the soft cheese, icing sugar and vanilla together with the lemon zest, if using, until smooth and thick, and chill to firm slightly.

6 Place the cake on a plate and swirl the frosting over the top. Decorate the top with a few walnut halves.

CITRUS DRIZZLE CUP CAKES

You can top these with just a spoonful of Lemon and lime curd (*see* page 193) or glacé icing. Just mix sifted icing sugar with a good squeeze of lemon juice and a dash of water, if necessary, to form a thick cream and spoon on top of the cooled cakes.

Makes 8

75g butter, softened
75g caster sugar
75g self-raising flour
¾ tsp baking powder
Finely grated zest and juice of ½ small lemon or 1 small
  lime

For the drizzle
3 tbsp lemon or lime juice (use bottled if you prefer)
3 tbsp caster sugar
A little grated lemon or lime zest (optional)

1 Beat the butter until soft and fluffy in a bowl, then add all
   the remaining ingredients for the cakes and beat well with a
   wooden spoon or electric whisk until fluffy and light.

2   Arrange 8 double-thickness paper cake cases round the edge of the metal tray (or a round baking sheet or ovenproof plate) on the turntable.

3   Cook on COMBINATION: CONVECTION 180°C + LOW/WARM (10 per cent) for 9–10 minutes or until risen and golden on top and the centres spring back when lightly pressed. Transfer to a wire rack. Remove the second paper cases and keep for another day.

4   To make the drizzle, mix the juice and sugar together and spoon over the cakes while still hot and decorate with a little lemon or lime zest, if using, then leave to cool.

DOUBLE CHOCOLATE BROWNIES

You can omit the white chocolate chips if you prefer plain chocolate brownies, or replace them with chopped walnuts to give a different flavour and texture.

Makes 12

A little sunflower oil, for greasing
150g butter, diced
115g plain chocolate, broken into pieces
300g caster sugar
4 large eggs, beaten
1 tsp natural vanilla extract
125g self-raising flour
25g cocoa powder
50g white chocolate chips (or chopped from a block)

1   Grease and line a 23 x 18cm shallow, microwave-safe, ovenproof dish or baking tin with baking paper so it stands at least 2cm above the dish.
2   Put the butter and chocolate in a microwave-safe bowl and place on the turntable. MICROWAVE on MEDIUM (50–60 per cent) for 2 minutes until nearly melted. Stir well to melt completely.

3 Mix in the sugar then beat in the eggs.

4 Stir in the remaining ingredients.

5 Spoon the brownie mixture into the prepared dish and smooth the surface.

6 Place on the metal tray or low rack on the turntable. Cook on COMBINATION: CONVECTION 190°C + MEDIUM for 5 minutes until risen and cracked on top but still a bit squidgy in the middle. Leave to cool in the dish then cut into pieces.

DATE, COCONUT AND CASHEW CHOCOLATE BOUNTY BARS

These are a more nutritious alternative to most chocolate biscuits, being packed with the goodness of oats, cashew nuts and dates. They're good energy bars when revising for exams, after strenuous exercise or just as a reviver after a busy day.

Makes 25

For the base
A little sunflower oil, for greasing
100g rolled oats
50g desiccated coconut, plus extra for dusting
1 tbsp cocoa powder
100g chopped dates
A pinch of salt
5 tbsp milk
100g butter, softened

For the topping
100g raw cashew nuts, soaked in 100ml hot water for
  30 minutes
150g chopped dates
50g raisins
75g butter
4 tbsp clear honey
1 tsp natural vanilla extract
150g good quality (70 per cent cocoa solids) chocolate

1 Grease and line a 20cm square shallow baking dish or tin with baking paper. Put the base ingredients except the butter in a food processor and blitz until crumbly. Add the butter and run the machine to form a paste.

2 Press the mixture into the prepared dish. Place on the metal tray or low rack on the turntable. Cook on COMBINATION: CONVECTION 180°C + MEDIUM-LOW/ SIMMER (25–30 per cent) for 10 minutes until just firm. Set aside to cool.

3 To make the filling, drain the cashew nuts, reserving the soaking water. Measure out 75ml of it and place in a microwave-safe bowl; add the dates and raisins. Place on the turntable and MICROWAVE ON HIGH (100 per cent) for 5 minutes until soft and the water has been absorbed. Stir in the butter until melted.

4 Blitz in a food processor with the softened cashews, honey and vanilla extract, stopping and scraping down the sides as necessary, until smooth.

5 Break up the chocolate and place in a microwave-safe bowl. MICROWAVE ON HIGH for 2 minutes, then stir until melted. Mix into the date and nut mixture. Spread over the base and sprinkle with a little more desiccated coconut. Chill until firm then cut into small squares to serve. Store any remaining in an airtight container in the fridge.

SHORTBREAD FINGERS

This shortbread is perfect with a cuppa or to serve as an accompaniment to ice cream, mousses or fruit desserts. It cooks quickly and evenly in your combination cooker. If you like a crisper texture, after combination cooking, remove the metal tray or rack and MICROWAVE on HIGH (100 per cent) for 3 minutes.

Makes 12 fingers

A little sunflower oil, for greasing
150g butter, softened
75g caster sugar, plus extra for dusting
150g plain flour
50g cornflour
A pinch of salt

1   Grease and line an 18 x 23cm shallow microwave-safe, ovenproof dish with baking paper.
2   Beat the butter and sugar together until light and fluffy. Sift the flour, cornflour and salt over, and work in with a wooden spoon to form a soft dough.
3   Press into the prepared dish in an even layer. Prick all over with a fork.
4   Place the metal tray or the low rack on the turntable. Cook on COMBINATION: 150°C + MEDIUM (50–60 per cent) for 5 minutes until pale gold.
5   Sprinkle with a dusting of caster sugar. Leave to cool in the dish for 10 minutes, then mark into 12 fingers. Leave to cool completely before cutting completely and removing from the dish. Store in an airtight container.

SAUCES AND SUNDRIES

Sauces make a huge difference to many a meal. Using your microwave means they are ready in next to no time and if needed, can be reheated quickly without dirtying a pan. Here are my favourites that can enhance many of your family's favourite meals. There is also an all-year-round apricot jam and a citrus curd that you can use to add zing to desserts as well as spreading on toast, bread, scones or crumpets.

HOLLANDAISE SAUCE

The secret is not to get over-excited and try to cook this even more quickly. If you do, the eggs will scramble and the sauce will not have the thick, shiny texture it should. The stopping and whisking is vital and it only takes about a minute and a half, which isn't very long!

Serves 4

115g butter
Lemon juice
2 eggs
A good pinch of cayenne
Salt and white pepper

1   Put the butter in a microwave-safe bowl. Cover with a sheet of kitchen paper to prevent spattering. MICROWAVE ON HIGH (100 per cent) for 50 seconds until nearly melted. Remove from the oven and stir until completely liquid.
2   Whisk in 1 tbsp lemon juice, the eggs and cayenne. Return to the microwave and MICROWAVE on HIGH for 20 seconds. Remove and whisk well. Continue in 10-second bursts, whisking well between each burst, until the mixture is thick, smooth and glossy.
3   Taste and add more lemon juice and salt and pepper as required.

QUICK BÉCHAMEL SAUCE

For an unflavoured white sauce, simply omit the bay leaf or bouquet garni and onion powder.

Makes about 300ml

20g butter
3 tbsp plain flour
300ml milk
1 bay leaf or a bouquet garni sachet (optional)
1 slice of onion (optional)
Salt and white pepper

1   Put the butter in a microwave-safe bowl and MICROWAVE on HIGH (100 per cent) for about 30 seconds until melted.
2   Whisk in the flour and milk until smooth and add the bay leaf or bouquet garni sachet, and onion, if using.
3   MICROWAVE on HIGH for 1 minute. Whisk, then continue to microwave in 1-minute bursts, whisking after each burst, until thickened and glossy (about 4 minutes).
4   Season to taste and discard the bay leaf or bouquet garni sachet and onion, if used.

VARIATIONS
Cheese sauce
Prepare as above but add 50g grated mature Cheddar cheese and ½ tsp English mustard, before seasoning.

Parsley sauce
Prepare as above but add 3 tbsp chopped fresh parsley after cooking, before seasoning to taste.

GRAVY-TO-GO

This is worth making to store in your freezer for those occasions when you want a tasty gravy but aren't cooking a joint or other meat that would have juices you can quickly turn into a meaty sauce. You can store the strained thin gravy at the end of step 3, ready to thicken when needed, if you prefer. This is also suitable for vegetarians. Adding the brandy turns the gravy into a delicious sauce for special-occasion meat or vegetarian dishes.

Makes about 300ml

Good knob of butter
1 onion, chopped
1 carrot, sliced
1 celery stick, chopped (or ½ tsp celery seeds)
350ml vegetable stock, made with stock concentrate
1 tbsp soy sauce
2 tsp tomato purée
1 bay leaf
2 tbsp plain flour
A pinch each of sugar and salt
Freshly ground black pepper
2 tsp brandy (optional)

1   Put the butter in a large bowl on the turntable. Cover with a sheet of kitchen paper and MICROWAVE on HIGH (100 per cent) for 20 seconds.

2 Add the prepared vegetables, stir, re-cover and MICROWAVE on HIGH for 5 minutes, stirring occasionally.

3 Add the stock, soy sauce, tomato purée and bay leaf. (Do not cover.) MICROWAVE on HIGH for 10 minutes. If time, leave to stand until cold, then strain; if not, strain straight away.

4 Blend the flour with a little of the strained gravy in the same or in a clean bowl. Stir in the remaining gravy until smooth. MICROWAVE on HIGH for 3 minutes, stirring occasionally, until thickened. Season to taste with the sugar, salt, pepper and the brandy, if using.

FRESH TOMATO SAUCE

This is a gorgeous sauce to use when summer tomatoes are at their peak. In winter, you can use 2 cans of chopped tomatoes instead. It's great with pasta, to smooth over pizza bases, as a side sauce with grills and fried fish, meat or poultry, or to smother a green vegetable such as broccoli before adding a béchamel or cheese sauce.

Serves 4—6

1 onion, chopped
1 garlic clove, crushed
2 tbsp olive oil
750g ripe tomatoes, roughly chopped
1 tsp caster sugar
1 tbsp tomato purée
Salt and freshly ground black pepper
1 bouquet garni sachet

1   Put the onion, garlic and olive oil in a large microwave-safe bowl, stir, then place on the turntable. MICROWAVE on HIGH (100 per cent) for 3 minutes to soften.

2   Add the remaining ingredients and stir again. MICROWAVE on HIGH for 12 minutes, stirring once or twice until pulpy. Discard the bouquet garni. Taste and re-season if necessary.

SALTED CARAMEL SAUCE

Serve this hot, drizzled over ice cream, over sweet pancakes, with profiteroles – you name it. It's a great sauce to have in your fridge and a delicious change from chocolate!

Makes about 300ml

120g granulated sugar
3 tbsp hot water
90g unsalted butter, diced
8 tbsp Greek yoghurt (don't use low-fat-style!)
1 tsp flaked sea salt

1   Put the sugar in a microwave-safe bowl. Add the water and stir briefly.
2   Place on the turntable and MICROWAVE on HIGH (100 per cent) for 5 minutes until the sugar caramelises to a mid-brown but is not too dark.
3   Remove from the oven and whisk in the butter until completely melted, then stir in the yoghurt and the salt. Use straight away or store in a clean screw-topped jar in the fridge and reheat as required, adding a little milk or water if too thick.

'REAL' CUSTARD

This is a cornflour-based sauce, but the addition of eggs whisked in gives a delicious 'real' custard flavour and texture.

Makes about 450ml

4 tbsp cornflour
450ml milk
1 tsp natural vanilla extract
2 tbsp caster sugar
2 eggs, beaten

1 Blend the cornflour into the milk in a microwave-safe measuring jug. Stir in the vanilla and sugar.
2 Place on the turntable and MICROWAVE on HIGH (100 per cent) for 3–4 minutes, stopping and whisking after every minute, until thick and smooth. Whisk in the beaten eggs. Return to the microwave and MICROWAVE on MEDIUM (50–60 per cent) for 1 minute only. Whisk again before serving.

LEMON AND LIME CURD

You can, of course, make all-lemon curd: simply use the rind and juice of 3 lemons and omit the limes.

Makes 2 jars

100g butter
225g caster sugar
Finely grated zest and juice of 1 large lemon
Finely grated zest and juice of 3 limes
4 eggs

1 Put the butter in a large microwave-safe basin and MICROWAVE ON HIGH (100 per cent) for 50 seconds to melt.
2 Beat in all the remaining ingredients, adding the eggs last.
3 MICROWAVE ON MEDIUM (50–60 per cent) for 5 minutes, whisking after every 30 seconds, until thick and glossy. It should coat the back of a spoon. Cook a little longer if still not thick enough, continuing in 30-second bursts.
4 Sterilise two jam jars (better than one large one as it will keep better): put about 2cm water in the clean jars and MICROWAVE ON HIGH for 3 minutes or until boiling. Carefully remove from the microwave using oven gloves and tip out the water. Drain upside down on kitchen paper to dry, then pour in the still-hot curd. Cover, label and leave to cool, then store in a cool place. Refrigerate after opening.

DRIED APRICOT JAM

This is simple jam to make in winter and spring when local fresh fruit is not available. The apricots retain a little texture after cooking, so you still have nice chunky pieces of fruit in each mouthful. It's also good with a large handful of blanched whole or flaked almonds thrown in at the same time as you add the sugar to add extra flavour and a delicious crunch. Make sure the bowl is less than a third full when you add the sugar or it will boil over when you cook it.

Makes 3 jars

300g dried apricots
450ml boiling water
600g preserving sugar
150ml lemon juice
Few drops of natural almond extract

1   Roughly chop the apricots, then place in a very large, microwave-safe bowl, pour over the boiling water and leave to soak for several hours or overnight.
2   When ready to make the jam, sterilise two clean jars. Put about 2cm of water in 2 or 3 jam jars and place on the turntable. MICROWAVE on HIGH (100 per cent) for 3 minutes or until the water is boiling. Remove from the oven using oven gloves. Pour the boiling water into a dish that will hold the jars side by side. Drain the jars upside down on kitchen paper for a minute or two then stand the jars right-way up in the water to keep them warm.

3   Place the bowl with the soaked apricots on the turntable and MICROWAVE on HIGH for about 10 minutes until really tender. Stir in the sugar, lemon juice and almond extract.

4   MICROWAVE on HIGH for 5 minutes, stirring once or twice, until the sugar has completely dissolved.

5   MICROWAVE on HIGH for a further 15 minutes, then test for a set. The temperature should reach 110°C on a sugar thermometer, or a little spooned onto a saucer and cooled should wrinkle when a finger is pushed through it. Alternatively, if you take up a spoonful of the jam, hold it above the bowl and let the jam drop back into the bowl, the last of it should hang in a jelly-like teardrop on the spoon. If not, microwave a little longer – it may take up to 20 minutes in total.

6   If the jars have cooled down completely, add a little boiling water to the dish holding them. Pour the hot jam into the warm jars and cover. Remove from the dish of water, dry the outsides of the jars, label and leave to cool. Store in a cool, dry place.

INDEX